Salman Rushdie's
Midnight's Children

CONTINUUM CONTEMPORARIES

Also available in this series:

· **SALMAN RUSHDIE'S**

Midnight's Children

A READER'S GUIDE

NORBERT SCHÜRER

continuum
NEW YORK · LONDON

2004

The Continuum International Publishing Group Inc
15 E 26 Street, New York, NY 10010

The Continuum International Publishing Group Ltd
The Tower Building, 11 York Road, London SE1 7NX

www.continuumbooks.com

Printed in the United States of America

Library of Congress Cataloging-in-Publication Data

Schürer, Norbert.
  Salman Rushdie's Midnight's children : a reader's guide / Norbert
Schürer.
      p.   cm.—(Continuum contemporaries)
  Includes bibliographical references and index.
  ISBN 0-8264-1575-X (pbk. : alk. paper)
  1. Rushdie, Salman. Midnight's children.   2. India—In literature.
I. Title.   II. Series.
PR6068.U757M5337   2004
823'.914—dc22   2004011877

Contents

The Novelist

The Fatwa

Salman Rushdie is probably best known across the world as the epicenter of the unfortunate episode called the Rushdie Affair. The author's fourth novel, *The Satanic Verses*, was published in the United Kingdom, where Rushdie was living (in London), on September 26, 1988. The book, which initially received mixed reviews in the British press, mainly treated the lives of two Indian immigrants to Britain named Gibreel Farishta and Saladin Chamcha; however, it also contained a character called Mahound, a literary incarnation of the Muslim Prophet Muhammad. This character is held up to significant ridicule in *The Satanic Verses*. For example, he visits brothels and gives his nine favorite prostitutes the names of the nine wives of the Prophet; he is motivated by politics rather than by faith; and he dictates his religious work to a scribe, who misunderstands him and introduces deviations to the sacred text. Furthermore, "Mahound" is the version of the Prophet's name that was used by Christian theologians in the Middle Ages who were less than sympathetic toward Islam. The title refers to an incident where the Prophet seems to endorse other gods next to Allah, but it turns out that the statement has been made by Satan. At the same time, all of this is narrated with considerable ironic distance: The story is presented as the crazy ramblings of a schizophrenic character.

Neither Muslims nor Christians in the United Kingdom expressed much opposition to the novel immediately after publication; rather, the first protest came from Syed Shahabuddin, a member of the Indian parliament, in late September. At Shahabuddin's request, India banned *The Satanic Verses* on October 5, 1988. From India, the furor over Rushdie's novel spread over the Muslim world—it was censored in Pakistan, Bangladesh, Saudi Arabia, Egypt, Indonesia, and other countries—and then back to the West. In January 1989, Muslims in Bradford, a town in British Yorkshire, organized a burning of the novel that was broadcast on television. Soon thereafter, a demonstration of Muslims upset by *The Satanic Verses* took place in London. Not all Muslims agreed with these actions, which were promoted by the more conservative and fundamentalist members of Islam both abroad and in Europe. In February 1989, riots developed from demonstrations against the novel in the Pakistani capitol, Islamabad, and in Indian Kashmir. The Iranian Ayatollah Ruhollah Khomeini, a Shia Muslim religious scholar (Imam) and leader of the Iranian political revolution that had deposed the dictator Reza Shah Pahlavi, apparently under the impression of these events, composed and pronounced a religious edict called a *fatwa* on Valentine's Day, February 14, 1989. Khomeini wrote:

I inform all zealous Muslims of the world that the author of the book entitled *The Satanic Verses*—which has been compiled, printed, and published in opposition to Islam, the Prophet, and the Qur'an—and all those involved in its publication who were aware of its content, are sentenced to death.

I call on all zealous Muslims to execute them quickly, wherever they may be found, so that no one else will dare to insult the Muslim sanctities. God willing, whoever is killed on this path is a martyr.

The news of the *fatwa* reached Rushdie as he was giving a television interview in London and did not stop him from attending the funeral of his friend Bruce Chatwin, the travel writer. After that event, he spent the afternoon in seclusion in the office of his London agent. Rushdie and his then-wife Marianne Wiggins then stayed under police protection at an apartment she used for writing. The following day, the British Special Branch—the equivalent of the U.S. Secret Service—offered to assist Rushdie. He accepted and went into hiding indefinitely.

It is difficult to answer the question of why *The Satanic Verses* offended many Muslims and why this offense translated into concrete action, and there are literally dozens of books addressing the topic. This debate unfortunately has long overshadowed the literary analysis of *The Satanic Verses*. Many aspects of the novel are clearly contrary to Islamic doctrine. Although challenges to Christian theology are generally considered acceptable in the West, similar challenges are not very common in the Muslim world. Pluralist Western societies (which can no longer really be called Christian) accommodate theological criticism in a way that Muslim societies do not. In other words, many Muslims see their religion as prescriptive and infallible, whereas there is little sense of inviolable standards in the West. For that reason, a critic in the West is merely a gadfly, whereas the same person in Islam is perceived as a heretical menace to society.

At the same time, most of the major players in the Rushdie Affair—including MP Shahabuddin and Ayatollah Khomeini—had by their own testimony not actually read *The Satanic Verses*. In addition, the *fatwa* seemed to be a power play in the struggle between more conservative and more progressive elements among Iranian politicians. In other words, Khomeini might have issued his edict in order to secure his political position against those who wanted to open and reform Iranian society. Finally, the extent to which the Ayatollah even had the authority to pronounce the *fatwa* remains unclear. Because Islam has no hierarchical structure as does, for example, the Catholic church, there is no one authority to whom all

Muslims are (at least theoretically) beholden. Instead, Khomeini was exploiting his position as a popular and successful leader to impose his personal interpretation on Muslim people across the globe.

In the ensuing years, Rushdie remained in hiding, apparently moving from one habitation to the next, at his own cost, over and over again. (There was and is debate over the cost of the *fatwa* to British taxpayers: Even though some detractors claim that the costs were more than £10 million, Rushdie maintains the costs were covered by his own tax payments.) Some of the other people named in the *fatwa* were not as lucky—the translator of Rushdie's novels into Japanese, Hitoshi Igarashi, was stabbed to death, and assassination attempts were made against the Norwegian publisher and Italian translator of *The Satanic Verses*. In all, about 60 people died as a result of the Rushdie Affair. Because of the responses to the novel, paperback publication was held up and finally only went forward with a consortium of presses. Authors across the world weighed in with comments on the Rushdie Affair. Writers—as well as politicians—predominantly sided with Rushdie, invoking the Western idea of the freedom of expression. On the other hand, some prominent literary figures questioned Rushdie's tact in writing his novel and suggested withdrawing the novel. Opinions were also split in the Muslim world: Although many groups supported the *fatwa*—the students at Tehran University even collected money to add to the bounty of several million dollars that was at this time on Rushdie's head—others argued that *The Satanic Verses* were not really an insult to Islam at all.

Rushdie kept writing during this time, and he kept agitating for support from governments as well as defending his views in such essays as "In Good Faith" and "Is Nothing Sacred?" On a personal level, the *fatwa* had some disastrous and difficult consequences for Rushdie: His marriage broke up, and, in depression, he published an essay in which he converted to Islam and renounced *The Satanic*

Verses, only to recant several weeks later. Some editions of *Imaginary Homelands* include this essay, "Why I Have Embraced Islam," whereas others do not. In 1990, Rushdie also published a children's book called *Haroun and the Sea of Stories*, which can easily be interpreted as his attempt to fictionalize his own predicament, but which really offers much more. His first trip abroad, and his first public event since the *fatwa*, took place in December 1991, when he made a surprise appearance at a Columbia University forum on free speech in New York. He released a booklet on *The Wizard of Oz* in March 1992 through the British Film Institute. Throughout this time, Rushdie was agitating with his own British government, as well as many foreign dignitaries, to exert pressure on Iran to revoke the *fatwa*. His efforts unfortunately were hampered by the fact that there were Western hostages being held in Lebanon, and that some governments believed those hostages would be in danger if the Iranian government was provoked. In 1992, while Rushdie was in America, he tried to meet with U.S. senators, but the administration of President Bush apparently exerted its own pressure to stop these meetings. In the end, Rushdie was able to see only a small group of senators, including Daniel Patrick Moynihan (a Democrat from New York) and Patrick Leahy (Democrat/Vermont). In 1993, however, Rushdie was able to meet with President Clinton, signaling a turn in Western governments' involvement in the Rushdie Affair. By 1995, he had visited many other countries, including Germany, Denmark, Norway, Finland, Ireland, the Czech Republic, Spain, and Canada. That year, he made his first *announced* public appearance with a book reading in Oxford. The new British government, Labor instead of Tory, seems to have been more concerned about the author's plight. Another three years later, the Iranian government declared an official end to the *fatwa*; unfortunately, there are still extremist Muslim groups trying to uphold the long-dead Ayatol-

lah Khomeini's edict, and they are offering a substantial bounty, so
Salman Rushdie continues to live under the shadow of assassination.

Before the Rushdie Affair

By the time Rushdie was thrust into the limelight by the *fatwa*, he
had already had a long and eventful life and career. As a matter of
fact, many aspects of his biography were integrated into his magnum
opus, *Midnight's Children*. Like his protagonist Saleem Sinai,
Ahmed Salman Rushdie was born around the time of India's independence. Whereas Saleem enters the world on that exact day, August 15, 1947, Rushdie was born two months earlier, on June 19,
1947, in Bombay. Now, he recalls that "it was a family joke that the
British left only two months after my arrival (Chauhan 32)." Like
Saleem, his parents had been married before. Rushdie's father was
Anis Ahmed Rushdie, a Muslim lawyer and businessman from
Delhi; his mother was Negin Butt, a teacher from northern India.
Anis Rushdie's father, Salman's grandfather (who died before he was
born), was a successful merchant as well as a minor Urdu poet who
moved the family into the Indian upper middle class, and who sent
his son Anis to study in Cambridge. Negin Butt's father was a doctor
who was officially Muslim, but he allowed his daughter to be edu-
cated and did not demand that she live in *purdah*, the traditional
female seclusion from the world practiced by many Muslims.

When Salman was a child, the Rushdie family—with three
younger daughters—lived in a colonialist estate called Windsor Villa
that certainly served as a model for *Midnight's Children*'s Methwold
Estate. Like Saleem, Salman had a nanny called Mary, who had
previously worked at the hospital where he was born. "According to
family legend, [she] took one look at him and decided she would
become this baby's ayah: in effect, his 'second mother (Hamilton

90).'" The author and his protagonist are also similar in that the young Salman believed he was the center of the universe. Today, Rushdie has an explanation for this perception: "Being the only son and eldest child in a middle-class Indian family does make you tend to think that the world revolves round you (Chauhan 3)." Rushdie was brought up bilingually in English and Urdu. Anis Rushdie was apparently a master storyteller who made up ongoing narratives in the fashion of the *Arabian Nights* from night to night. The family was technically Muslim, but they did not observe many Muslim rites or festivals—and for that reason did not seriously consider leaving India after Partition, the division of the British colony India into predominantly Hindu India and predominantly Muslim Pakistan in 1947. Rushdie lists *The Wizard of Oz* as his earliest literary influence and names "Heartbreak Hotel" as his first rock-n-roll record. He claims he knew he wanted to be a writer from an early age.

After attending the Cathedral and John Connon School in Bombay as an outstanding pupil, the first major change in Salman Rushdie's life came when he was sent to England in 1961 to continue his education—a kind of exile not unlike Saleem's various adventures outside his home. Rushdie was sent to Rugby, a prominent private school ("public" in British terms) known for its conservative values. Even though he was smart, Rushdie did not fit in, perhaps because he was bad at sports, and he does not have fond memories of this period of his life. He believes "it was the triple whammy: foreign, clever, bad at games (Reder 219)." His worst moment was trying to eat a kipper, the British meal of smoked fish (herring or salmon), on his first day without any help. Later, he recollects such racial attacks as a classmate writing the phrase, "Wogs Go Home," on his door. (*Wog* is a British slang word for a dark-skinned foreigner, particularly of Asian descent.) Even though Rushdie physically assaulted the author and brought overt racial slurs to an end, he never felt fully accepted. Whereas some of his classmates have claimed not to recall such events, the difference in memory might very well be due to the fact that they were never subject to such racism. In any case, even at this early age, Rushdie was pushed into a role that he has inhabited ever since: part insider as a student at an elite educational institution, part outsider as an embattled racial minority.

In 1962, while Rushdie was at Rugby, his family had sold their possessions in India—a move that Rushdie says made him very angry—and followed him to England. Two years later, Anis Rushdie decided to move the Rushdies to Karachi, so when Salman graduated in 1965 he came to a new family residence, where he did not at all feel at home. In addition, this was the time of one of several military confrontations between India and Pakistan, and Rushdie felt caught in the middle: He lived in Pakistan and felt some loyalty to the country (not to mention physically threatened by Indian bombs), but his history was intimately connected with India. He was fortunately able to save himself from this wrenching situation by returning to England: After some thought, he had chosen to follow his father's footsteps and attend King's College in Cambridge. As Rushdie has written, "It was a very good time to be at Cambridge (Hamilton 96)," because the years from 1965 to 1968 were the heyday of what is now generically referred to as "the Sixties." In that spirit, Rushdie apparently did not spend much time on his studies; rather, he went to the movies almost every day and performed in a number of student drama productions. He did take one class in his final year that was to prove significant: He pursued an independent study with Arthur Hibbert on Muhammad and the rise of Islam.

After graduating from King's College with a mediocre degree, Rushdie went to Karachi to work for television there; however, the atmosphere proved to be too censorious, so he returned to London and tried to be a professional actor at the experimental Oval House theater. When that career was failing, Rushdie embarked on his first novel and successively took part-time jobs at two advertising firms:

Sharp MacManus and Ogilvy & Mather. Around this time, he met his first wife, Clarissa Luard. The two were married in April 1976 and had their only son, Zafar, in 1979. They separated in 1985 after Australian author Robyn Davidson became Rushdie's new partner. He and Clarissa divorced officially in 1987. By that time, Rushdie had met and moved in with American author Marianne Wiggins, who left and maligned him during the Rushdie Affair.

Rushdie's first novel, *Grimus*, was published somewhat serendipitously when the author failed to win a competition for a science fiction novel, but aroused the interest of Liz Calder, an editor at the publisher Victor Gollancz. Calder purchased the novel, and with the money he earned from the sale Rushdie and Luard went on a five-month trip to the Indian subcontinent in 1975, during which *Midnight's Children* was born. Rushdie published only one novel, *Shame*, between the publication of *Midnight's Children* and the Rushdie Affair. *Shame* is a fictionalized history of Pakistan (and thus, if only vaguely, similar to the previous book). At the same time, he became well known as a literary and political activist. His essays, particularly "Imaginary Homelands" and "Outside the Whale," established him as a prominent postcolonial critic (i.e., one who raised the problematic issue of the influence of the Western literary tradition on writing coming out of the Third World). In person and in print, Rushdie engaged with many other writers and critics addressing the same issues, such as Günter Grass, Edward Said, V.S. Naipaul, Nadine Gordimer, Graham Greene, Kazuo Ishiguro, Mario Vargas Llosa, and Gabriel García Márquez. Most of these essays, interviews, and introductions were later reprinted in *Imaginary Homelands*. Rushdie saw it as his duty as a writer to compose political criticism as well, sparing no punches against heads of states he considered bad for their countries, like Margaret Thatcher and Indira Gandhi. In 1986, Rushdie visited Nicaragua and for the first time encountered a government he actually liked in the Sandinista revolution. His experiences and conclusions were written down in *The*

Jaguar Smiles. In 1987, on the fortieth anniversary of Indian Independence, Rushdie went to India and produced a documentary called "The Riddle of Midnight," which is about the "real" Midnight's Children.

Since the Rushdie Affair

In terms of setting, Rushdie's fictional career started in the unreal country of science fiction with *Grimus* and moved to the Indian subcontinent with *Midnight's Children* and *Shame*. In both of these novels, cultural hybridity and purity were major issues, and Rushdie continued to explore that topic in his subsequent novels. The settings of Rushdie's fiction were already migrating during the time of the Rushdie Affair. In 1994, he published a collection of short stories titled, *East, West*, that indicated the direction in which he was moving. Rushdie published *The Moor's Last Sigh* the following year. Much of that book was set in Spain (among other things, the title referred to the departure of the Moors from Spain in 1492). A reading on the promotional tour for this novel was the first publicly announced event Rushdie attended since the *fatwa*. The book was short-listed for the Booker Prize and won the Whitbread Prize, another important British literary award.

At the same time, Rushdie had not forgotten India and *Midnight's Children*. In 1996, he worked on a script for a television adaptation of *Midnight's Children*; the following year he co-edited an anthology of Indian writing since Independence with his partner Elizabeth West, whom he had met in 1994 and married in August 1997, before their son Milan was born. The preface to the anthology, titled *The Vintage Book of Indian Writing, 1947–1997* in the United Kingdom and *Mirrorworks: 50 Years of Indian Writing, 1947–1997* in the United States and published on the fiftieth anniversary of Independence, was controversial because it argued that the best Indian writing of the past half century was all in English. The next year was momentous for Rushdie because the *fatwa* was officially withdrawn by the Iranian government. He has written retrospectively about the effects of the Rushdie Affair:

When asked about the effect on my writing of the ten-year-long assault upon it, I've answered lightheartedly that I've become more interested in happy endings; and that, as I've been told that my recent books are my funniest, the attacks have evidently improved my sense of humor. . . . I am conscious of shifts in my writing. There was always a tug-of-war in me between "there" and "here," the pull of roots and of the road. In that struggle of insiders and outsiders, I used to feel simultaneously on both sides. Now I've come down on the side of those who by preference, nature, or circumstance simply do not belong. This unbelonging—I think of it as *disorientation*, loss of the East—is my artistic country now. Wherever my books find themselves, by a favored armchair, near a hot bath, on a beach, or in a late-night pool of bedside light: that's my only home. (*SATL* 265–67)

In 1999, Rushdie changed his own life in three significant ways that can be interpreted as expressing a new outlook on life. First, he had an operation for ptosis, a medical condition that for a long time had not allowed him to raise his eyelids fully and might have eventually led to blindness. While the ptosis had given him a distinctive appearance, after the operation Rushdie was, in the literal as well as the metaphorical sense, able to take a new look at the world. At the same time, Rushdie moved from London to New York, explaining that he found London's literary scene "backbiting and incestuous" (Max 68) and characterizing New York as "a Western rewrite of Bombay" (Max 69) because of its cosmopolitanism. With the move to New York, Rushdie also split from his wife Elizabeth West and began a relationship with the Indian model Padma Lakshmi. The year 1999 also saw the publication of the novel, *The Ground Beneath*

Her Feet, which fictionalized the career of a rock band based on the ancient Greek myth of Orpheus and Eurydice and had the characters moving from India to London and finally to New York. This was Rushdie's first novel concentrating almost exclusively on popular culture and set in contemporary times. The same year, Rushdie began contributing columns to the *New York Times* on a variety of cultural and political topics, many of which are collected in *Step Across This Line*. In addition, Rushdie's *Haroun and the Sea of Stories* was turned into a play by the same team that was to tackle *Midnight's Children* later.

The third millennium proved to be new for Rushdie because in April, he returned to India for the first time since the *fatwa* with his son Zafar, an experience movingly recorded in the essay "A Dream of Glorious Return." Even though most of the visit went smoothly, Rushdie's reception at the ceremony for the Commonwealth Writers Prize in Delhi was quite riotous—J.M. Coetzee won the prize, but Rushdie received just as much or more media attention. In many ways, Rushdie was now as much a celebrity as an author, which might also be reflected in his appearances in such movies as *Dirty Pictures* (2000) and *The Diary of Bridget Jones* (2001). Of course, these cameos are hardly surprising considering the interest in cinema expressed in *Midnight's Children*. Still, he did not appear in a character role, as in his days in London in the late Sixties, but as himself. Rushdie started working on a project of four novels around this time connected only by theme—two with contemporary settings, one medieval tale, and one science fiction story. The first of these four to be published will probably be the forthcoming medieval tale, *The Enchantress of Florence*.

Just as Rushdie believed life was returning to normal, a devastating terrorist attack hit his new hometown on September 11, 2001. Earlier that year, he had published his latest novel, *Fury*, to mixed reviews. Many critics complained that the novel was no more than

a superficial fictionalization of Rushdie's own life because the protagonist is a middle-aged Indian who has become famous because of
his own creation and who has left his wife and child behind in London. At the same time, *Fury* was recognized as a literary homage to
New York, and it was accepted as that after 9/11. It is ironic that the
Toronto Globe & Mail newspaper had reported that Rushdie had
been banned from Air Canada flights that same day because he represented a security risk. In the aftermath of 9/11, Rushdie wrote one
of his syndicated columns expressing his love for New York and de-
fiance in the face of terrorism. He distinguished been Muslims in
general and the terrorists who perpetrated the attack, and he supported military action against the terrorists, but said that it had to be
supplemented by civilian action. At the end of his essay, Rushdie
wrote:

The fundamentalist believes that we believe in nothing. In his worldview,
he has absolute certainties, while we are sunk in sybaritic indulgences. To
prove him wrong, we must first know that he is wrong. We must agree on
what matters: kissing in public places, bacon sandwiches, disagreement,
cutting-edge fashion, literature, generosity, water, a more equitable distribu-
tion of the world's resources, movies, music, freedom of thought, beauty,
love. These will be our weapons. Not by waging war, but by the unafraid
way we choose to live shall we defeat them (*SATL* 33).

These sentiments made Rushdie popular in New York, but he was
criticized in the United Kingdom for stirring up the Muslim community again with these and other remarks. Rushdie, however, still
maintains an apartment in London and visits frequently. His latest
literary endeavor, a dramatic adaptation of *Midnight's Children*, was
put on by the British Royal Shakespeare Company in 2003, but also
visited the United States for a short run. At one point Rushdie apparently tried to convince the British Council to organize a tour of the
production to Pakistan. Thus, he remains an author between continents.

2

The Novel

The main difficulty in reading *Midnight's Children*, and in writing about it, is that the book is encyclopedic and overwhelming. Rushdie's novel covers more than sixty years in the history of three countries on the Indian subcontinent, and there are more characters—with strange and changing names—than in most works of fiction. Rushdie seems to assume that his readers have a working knowledge of Hindu mythology, and there are implicit and explicit references to major works of literature in the Western tradition. In addition, any narrative or historical statements in the book have to be questioned critically because the narrator—by his own admission—is unreliable. Furthermore, the readers are teased with moments of foreshadowing, whereas major plot revelations are deferred almost indefinitely, and all of this is mixed with fantastical elements. These features somehow come together to develop the issues of the novel, which include a confrontation of East and West, an interrogation of the concept of nation, an assessment of the first thirty years of Indian history, a questioning of notions of gender, an examination of the idea of personal identity, a challenge to the literary form of the novel, an argument with traditional versions of history and historiography, and an analysis of the certain models of culture.

In all this, it needs to be clear that there is not just *one* point. Rushdie himself recalls an amusing experience after the publication of his novel:

I went on a lecture tour to India . . . and I remember in Delhi a girl said to me, "Look, I've read your book, this *Midnight's Children*; it's very long, but I read it." And then she said, "What I want to know is: what's your point?" To my reply, "Do I really have to have just one point?" she answered, "Yes, of course. I know what you're going to say. You're going to say the whole book is the point from the beginning to the end, aren't you?" "Yes," I said. "I thought so," she said. "It won't do" ("*Midnight's Children* and *Shame*" 2).

Still, to help his readers move from the often consciously juxtaposed and apparently mutually exclusive elements to overall meanings, Rushdie offers a significant organizing plot device that helps make sense of *Midnight's Children*: It is told as the autobiography of the first thirty years in the life of one Saleem Sinai, sitting in a pickle factory in Bombay and talking to his partner or muse Padma. As Saleem explains on the first page, he is "handcuffed to history," so throughout the novel he draws parallels between his own life and the continent he dwells on—Lewis gives an extensive parallel of fictional and historical events. The book is furthermore organized into thirty chapters, each of which is compared with a pickle jar by Saleem and (vaguely) parallels one of the years in his life.

The very first paragraph of *Midnight's Children* introduces at least three genres of discourse: autobiography, fairy tale, and history. Because the passage is repeated almost verbatim several times throughout the novel (e.g., 21/337 and 28/482), these genres must

be quite important. In this first instance, the narrator Saleem Sinai
writes:

I was born in the city of Bombay . . . once upon a time. No, that won't do,
there's no getting away from the date: I was born in Doctor Narlikar's Nursing Home on August 15th, 1947. And the time? The time matters, too. Well
then: at night. No, it's important to be more . . . On the stroke of midnight,
as a matter of fact. Clock-hands joined palms in respectful greeting as I
came. Oh, spell it out, spell it out: at the precise instant of India's arrival at
independence, I tumbled forth into the world (1/3).

First, Saleem indicates to his readers that they will be hearing a
chronological story of his life because he starts with his birth. Loca-
tion also appears to be important because Saleem specifies the loca-
tion Bombay (and later Doctor Narlikar's Nursing Home) before
getting to a date. The place is connected to society because the
"joined palms in respectful greeting" are a gesture associated with
Indian cultures. At the same time, however, Saleem gives a hint that
there is something less than straightforward about his story by invoking the fairy tale formula, "once upon a time." He speaks in conver-
sational language, chiding himself for giving insufficient
information, asking and answering questions, not finishing sentences, and using informal words. The language of the passage further adds significance by introducing an element of repetition (i.e.,
the word *no* is repeated several times), by alluding to the importance
of style (e.g., "spell it out"), and by using a shift in the meaning of an
individual word (e.g., *matter* is first a question of significance, then
a question of factuality or truth). It is most significant, however, that
Saleem finally spills the beans about the exact moment he is born
(even if he does not get back to that moment for more than 100
pages): the stroke of midnight on August 15, 1947, the moment of
India's independence from its former colonial occupier Great Brit-

ain. While Saleem takes his first breath and gets moved from one bed to another by his nurse, Mary Pereira, Jawaharlal Nehru is giving his famous "Tryst with Destiny" speech about India's historical mission, which Rushdie quotes at some length (8/129).

[It is unfortunate that the chapters are not numbered in any edition of *Midnight's Children*. In order to make references in the following text easier to trace in the various editions of the novel, however, I will give chapter as well as a page numbers from the most recent U.S. (Penguin) edition. For instance, 28/484 refers to the last page in the chapter, "A Wedding," in the Penguin edition.]

Pre-Independence History

More than just the birth of Saleem, *Midnight's Children* as a whole hinges on the exact point in time of India's independence. For one thing, the novel starts about 30 years before Independence, and symmetrically ends 30 years after it. (In the language of the region, many significant historical and political events are referred to in capitalized terms, such as *Partition* or *Emergency*.) It also needs to be noted that Independence does not refer just to India; rather, it also refers to the other country on the Subcontinent, Pakistan, which gained its freedom as a country at the same time. (The Subcontinent refers to the geographical entity of the Indian subcontinent, which today includes the countries India, Pakistan, and Bangladesh, as well as the disputed territory, Kashmir.) In addition, however, the moment of the birth of Saleem—offered in the book's first paragraph—is important because it signals to the reader that actual historical events will be important throughout the novel.

Midnight's Children begins chronologically in 1915, the year Saleem's grandfather Aadam Aziz returns from Europe to India, or, more specifically, Kashmir. The narrative indicates that this is a time of beginnings for Aadam by emphasizing that he hits his nose "in the early spring," when "the world was new again" (1/4). The year 1915 was historically the year two moderate leaders of the movement for Indian independence (i.e., Gopal Krishna Gokhale and Pherozeshah Mehta) died, making way for a more radical leadership to intensify the struggle. It was also the year Mohandas Karamchand "Mahatma" Gandhi returned to India. At the same time, the First World War was going on in Europe, with about two million Indians participating. On the day World War I ended, in one of many "historical coincidences" (2/23), Aadam's future wife, Naseem, develops a headache that allows him to see her face through the perforated sheet—World War I, Rushdie suggests, paves the way for India to gain its own face or identity.

In the 1920s, the Indian National Congress, a political party usually known simply as Congress, was agitating for some form of autonomy for what was then a British colony. In the concept of "Satyagraha" (4/63) or "holding on to the truth," Mahatma Gandhi discovered a form of nonviolent resistance (e.g., not accepting British awards, withdrawing from British schools, not paying rents to British or Indian landlords, challenging the British monopoly in salt) that initially proved very successful; however, successive British colonial administrations were also quite savvy in exploiting the conflicting aims of the movement (e.g., colonial autonomy or complete independence, cooperation with the British or confrontation) and managed to drag out the process for more than thirty years. Much of this time proved to be quite violent as well; for instance, when an intended show of strength turned into a sign of the weakness of colonial rule: In 1919, the British administration was trying to curb revolutionary sentiment and banned all political meetings. When one took place anyway in the Punjabi town of Amritsar at the Jallianwala Bagh bazaar, British General Reginald Dyer marched into the enclosed space with Indian troops and opened fire without provocation, killing 370 innocent people and wounding another one thousand. Aadam Aziz, who is present at the event, survives only because he falls over from a sneeze. Rushdie, who changes such historical details as the nationality of the soldiers involved, uses the massacre to point out how different individuals and traditions interpret history differently: While Aadam is horrified by the slaughter, Dyer is quoted as saying, "We have done a jolly good thing" (2/34).

Another movement arose during the same period that was based more on religious categories. Although Congress had originally been nonreligious, it soon attracted mostly Hindus, and in the 1920s and 1930s the Muslim League rose to prominence. From the 1930s Congress pretty much represented the Hindus, the League the Muslims of India. Although there were parts of the country where one group or the other was in the majority, there were no regions that were purely Hindu or Muslim, which made matters more difficult. The leader of the League, Mohammad Ali Jinnah, whom Ahmed Sinai does not trust (6/91), had negotiated a Congress–League pact with Gandhi in 1916, but the demands of the two groups subsequently drifted apart. By 1940, when the Second World War had started and it was fairly clear that the British would eventually leave India, the League decided they wanted a separate country for Muslims and invented the acronym Pakistan for it, made up of the letters of the predominantly Muslim regions of India. (Others, however, claim that Pakistan means "Land of the Pure" [20/328].) In *Midnight's Children*, the Muslim League makes an indirect appearance as an organization that Aadam Aziz loathes (3/46). As far as Muslim politics go, the novel invents the Free Islam Convocation, a group that wants to promote Muslim ideas, but within the framework of *one* India. This program can historically be associated with the early career of Jinnah, or with the Muslim Conference founded by Sheikh Mohamad Abdullah in Kashmir in 1932, but its leaders

Mian Abdullah, known as the Hummingbird, and Nadir Khan are fictions (3/39).

To complicate things further, there were at least two more issues in the political debates over the future of India: the Sikhs and the rulers of the small states in India, the maharajas. For one thing, as the Subcontinent was being partitioned between Hindus and Muslims, the third largest religion, Sikhism, was going empty-handed. Though less than 2 percent of the Indian population, that was a significant number, and the Sikhs were geographically concentrated in the Punjab. In *Midnight's Children*, this group only makes brief appearances, such as the "Sikh from the bicycle-repair shop [who] had had his turban pushed off his head" (3/39). Second, in its entire colonial occupation, Great Britain had technically never consolidated its rule over the Subcontinent, but left some states with a fair degree of autonomy and governed by maharajas (kings or princes). Although many of these were insignificant, others were important for political or economic reasons. Kashmir was probably most important of all. It was where a Hindu maharaja led a mostly Muslim population. In Rushdie's novel, this group is represented by the Rani of Cooch Naheen (*Rani* means princess or queen; Cooch Naheen is a fictional region similar to the Bengali Cooch Beehar, and *Naheen* means *nothing*). Like many of her historical counterparts, the Rani is interested in "cross-cultural concerns" between Indian and the British, which shows in that she "was going white in blotches" (3/45). Rushdie apparently implies that these high-class Indians were becoming too Anglicized and not paying enough attention to the concerns of their country people.

The British sent a number of viceroys, governor-generals, and other emissaries, many of whom are mentioned in *Midnight's Children*, into this mix. The most important British prime ministers at the time were Winston Churchill (in office 1940–45) and Clemens Attlee (1945–51; 5/69). The viceroy, or main representative of the

British government, was Lord Archibald Percival Wavell (1943–47), who was replaced by Earl Mountbatten. The anecdotes that Rushdie offers about Mountbatten installing a countdown calendar on his wall (6/100) and about his wife, "who ate chicken breasts secretly behind a locked lavatory door" (5/69), have their basis in fact.

Post-Independence History

Gandhi, Jinnah, and Mountbatten ultimately agreed to divide the Subcontinent into two states: mostly Hindu India and mostly Muslim Pakistan. At this time, in 1947, the Indian subcontinent had a population of approximately 411 million people (i.e., around 339 million in what was to become India, 72 million in Pakistan). Of the total, approximately 66% (i.e., 270 million) were Hindus. In addition, there were about 97 million Muslims (24%), 6.7 million Christians (1.6%), and 6 million Sikhs (1.5%).

India, however, merely acceded to the demands of the Muslim leaders and still considered itself a secular state; in contrast, Pakistani leaders believed in the "two-nation theory," according to which the Subcontinent was divided by religion. In part because of this conflict, in part because Mountbatten's preparations were insufficient, in part because neither solution considered the wishes of the Sikhs, and in part because the maharajas were allowed simply to choose whether they wanted to join India or Pakistan, the horror known now as Partition ensued after Independence on August 15, 1947 (i.e., Saleem's birthday). The Punjab region was divided between the two countries, leaving the Sikhs an even smaller minority in both. As a form of "ethnic cleansing" ensued with Hindus forcing Muslims to leave for Pakistan and Muslims compelling Hindus to move to India, militant Sikhs contributed to making the situation even more violent. Similar events happened across the country, with as many as one million people dying. The most horrific images of the period were trains of refugees arriving in either Pakistan or India—with all the passengers killed by terrorists on the other side. The Sinai family in *Midnight's Children* is unusual in that they stay in Indian Bombay even though they are Muslims, and Ahmed Sinai feels the wrath of Hindus over the years in attempts to freeze his assets or to drive him to emigrate. Altogether, more than twelve million people were displaced in some form around 1947.

The most enduring legacy of Partition, however, was the situation in Kashmir, the only princely state to border both new countries. Here, the Hindu maharaja had not chosen whether to cede his mostly Muslim country to India or Pakistan. Because the Pakistani government believed in the two-nation theory, they thought Kashmir should become a part of their country; because India wanted to follow established procedure, they waited for the maharaja to choose. In late 1947, Pakistan took matters into its own hands and invaded Kashmir; the maharaja responded by asking India for assistance, which soon secured most parts of the country. The boatman Tai dies in this battle "standing between the opposing forces and giving them a piece of his mind" (2/35). Jawaharlal Nehru, the new prime minister of India and a Kashmiri himself, promised to hold a referendum to determine the fate of the region, but that vote never happened, and Kashmir is still divided today. Because Kashmir embodies so many of the conflicts of India (i.e., religion, politics, culture, class) Rushdie sets the beginning and end of *Midnight's Children* there.

After 1947, India and Pakistan developed in different directions. For the most part India prospered under the leadership of Nehru, experiencing progress under two Five-Year Plans adopted from the Soviet models by the somewhat socialist Congress. The development of agriculture was promoted from 1951 to 1956; industry was the focus from 1956 to 1961. In contrast, Pakistan had a hard time.

Mohammad Jinnah died just a year after Independence in September 1948 and was followed by a series of serious but fairly incompetent leaders. The country was further disadvantaged by the fact that it was divided into two large sections, East and West Pakistan, that were separated by more than 1,000 miles of Indian territory and were very different in their economic and cultural makeup. Finally, although the country had been founded on the premise of Muslim identity, the extent to which that identity should be enshrined in government was unclear. A constitution was passed in 1956, but was subjected to what Saleem calls "gradual erosion" because of "faction strife and the multiple incompetences of Mr. Ghulam Mohammed" (20/329), the country's governor-general. In addition, the military was taking a larger and larger role in government, culminating in the coup of General Ayub Khan on October 27, 1958, which is described in the chapter, "Movements Performed by Pepperpots" (20/323–36).

At the same time and throughout the 1960s, rebellion was fermenting in East Pakistan under the Awami League and its leader Sheikh Mujib, opposed by Zulfikar Ali Bhutto and the Pakistan People's Party (24/399). Fighting broke out in early 1971 between the Awami League and the Pakistani army, although it remains unclear who instigated it. On March 25, Sheikh Mujib "proclaimed the state of Bangladesh" (24/409), which means country of the Bengals. The Indian army subsequently intervened and helped secure Bangladesh's independence. This, of course, is the conflict where Saleem—as the Buddha—works with the Canine Unit for Tracking and Intelligence Activities of the Pakistani army (the acronym CUTIA meaning *bitch*) and goes to the freshwater swamps called Sundurbans at the mouth of the Ganges with three soldiers.

Back in India, the country had engaged in a series of wars. In 1962, the government—still under Nehru—resolved to confront the Chinese, who were occupying a small part of Kashmir. On September 9, the day Ahmed Sinai suffers from a stroke, India decided to go to war. Rushdie characterizes this moment as another beginning by invoking the exact words of the beginning of the book: "And the time? The time matters, too. Well then: in the afternoon" (21/337). The Chinese army, however, easily defeated the Indian forces, and, on November 21 (i.e., the day of the draining of Saleem's nose) declared a unilateral ceasefire. There were also constant conflicts with Pakistan. For instance, Saleem contends that "it is my firm conviction that the hidden purpose of the Indo–Pakistani war of 1965 was nothing more nor less than the elimination of my benighted family from the face of the earth" (23/386), whereas more conventional historiography believes that the conflict arose from unresolved issues in Kashmir.

Most important to *Midnight's Children*, however, is certainly the Emergency declared in 1975 by Indira Gandhi, the Widow of the novel. Dhar has written an entire book about the Emergency. Nehru had ruled India until his death in 1964, and he was followed by Lal Bahadur Shastri for two years (23/374). In 1966, Shastri unexpectedly died of a heart attack, and with elections coming up Congress decided to put Nehru's daughter, Indira, in his position. Married to a doctor with the last name Gandhi, but not related to Mahatma—as Rushdie writes in his short biography (28/484)—Indira Gandhi had served as her father's hostess and as a minister in Shastri's government, but was not supposed to be a strong leader in her own right. She consolidated her power base, however, and easily won two elections. The second of those, in 1971, was challenged on the grounds of electoral corruption, and in 1975 the Allahabad High Court declared it invalid (28/479). In response, Gandhi first resigned, but then recanted and instead declared a state of emergency. The thirteen days between those two events are the days during which Parvati goes through labor and finally gives birth to Saleem/Shiva's son

Aadam (28/479–82). Rushdie calls the ensuing two years "a continuing midnight" (28/482).

In *Midnight's Children*, this Emergency is an unmitigated disaster and leads to a number of infringements on human rights. Rushdie is historically correct in his depiction of two major campaigns undertaken under the Emergency: the clearing of slums (29/493) and the sterilization of many Indians, both partly voluntary (Rushdie also wrote a wonderful short story called "The Free Radio" on sterilization) and partly by force (29/503). Population control was certainly necessary in a country with 600 million citizens—the number of particles into which Saleem dissolves on the last page of *Midnight's Children* (30/533)—but sterilization by force after two children did not go over well. Once again, Saleem is convinced that political events happen for his benefit: "Yes, Padma, Mother Indira really had it in for me" (28/484). The novel is also right in attributing a large part in both of these campaigns to Gandhi's son Sanjay, who was the heir apparent to the dynasty and reigned supreme in spite of not holding elected office. Furthermore, historians agree that Indira Gandhi was motivated to impose the Emergency not just to save India, but also to secure her own political survival. Martial law and luck, however, also conspired to make the years 1975–77 prosperous for India: Workers came to their offices on time, agricultural production reached an all-time high, and industry grew. Furthermore, Gandhi did not establish a permanent dictatorship; rather, she returned the country to democratic rule and even accepted the election results when she was ousted from office in 1977. Saleem returns to Kashmir and apparently dies shortly thereafter.

Names

In addition to historical facts, *Midnight's Children* demands extensive cultural knowledge for a better understanding. This knowledge takes on different forms and is conveyed on different levels throughout the novel: Some is explicitly elaborated, some is implicitly assumed, and some is difficult to discern for anyone but the specialist reader. Rushdie apparently does not believe that every reader needs to catch every allusion, but includes references to increase his novel's depth and to add resonances. Cultural knowledge of course also adds significantly to the overall theme of East versus West, or European versus Indian culture in *Midnight's Children*.

On one fairly obvious level, names are chosen with important cultural resonances—both from the Indian and from European traditions. Saleem claims, "Our names contain our fates" (21/348), and here these "speaking" names tell the reader about the novel's characters, or set up ironic distances between character (in the sense of person) and character (in the sense of personality). In addition, the Reverend Mother apparently randomly drops the word/phrase *whatsitsname* into conversation—nine times on one page alone (3/42)—perhaps indicating the importance of names. In alphabetical order, here are some of the first and last names and their possible significances:

Aadam Aziz: As the novel starts with beginnings, Saleem's grandfather takes his name from the first human being according to the Jewish Torah, the Christian Bible, and the Muslim Qur'an. Aadam's last name is a nod to the main Indian character in *A Passage to India*, E. M. Forster's seminal novel on India. The reference might signify that that like Forster's Dr. Aziz, Aadam is westernized, or that he has strong connections to Europe. In both Aadam and Saleem's names, Rushdie seems fond of alliteration, which could simply be employed for the sound effect, or be meant to imply repetition on a historical scale.

Ahmed: Saleem's father has an Arabic name that means "praiseworthy." In his energy and inventiveness, Ahmed certainly deserves praise, yet he also slaps his son, ignores his wife, and falls prey to alcoholism and despair.

Amina: Ahmed Sinai's wife's name means "honest woman," but then again, this is only the name she takes after her first life and marriage as Mumtaz ("jewel") fail. Even then, Amina is hardly honest, engaging in an extra-marital affair. At the same time, Amina is the name of the Muslim prophet Muhammad's mother—as she is of Saleem in *Midnight's Children.*

Naseem: The name of Aadam's wife means "breeze, fresh air." This name is certainly ironic in a character more frequently referred to in the novel as Reverend Mother, and who in many ways (e.g., sexual intercourse) represents that tradition against which her husband is fighting.

Padma: As Rushdie explains when he first introduces this character, Padma is "named for the lotus goddess, whose most common appellation amongst village folk is 'The One Who Possesses Dung'" (2/20). This goddess is also known as Lakshmi. (In a strange coincidence that even Rushdie could not have predicted, his current wife is a model called Padma Lakshmi.) *Padma* actually means *dung*, which might indicate the character's low class status, but also hints at the fact that something as lowly as manure can produce something as beautiful as a lotus.

Parvati: In Hindu mythology, Parvati (meaning "daughter of the mountain") is one of the most significant goddesses. She is married to Shiva and has two children, Ganesh and Skanda. Other names for Parvati are Uma and Kali. When Parvati in *Midnight's Children* dies, she is not really gone because Durga is another of her names. In mythology, Parvati and Shiva have a son, Ganesh, who ends up with an elephant's head. The son of the two in Rushdie's novel similarly has "ears so colossally huge that . . . they had thought, for one bad moment, that it was the head of a tiny elephant" (28/482).

Saleem Sinai: Arabic Saleem means "healthy, safe," which is quite ironic, especially if one considers his disaster-prone youth, during which he loses a finger, becomes half deaf, has hair torn out, walks bow-legged, and constantly has a runny nose. Rushdie points out similarities between his name and his protagonist's—"Saleem and Salman are after all, if you look back etymologically, kind of versions of the same name, and Rushdie and Sinai are names which derive from two different great Arab philosophers" (*Midnight's Children* 12)—strengthening the autobiographical connection between author and character. Saleem himself gives a paragraph-long analysis of Sinai (21/348f.). The last name's reference to the Biblical mountain is probably meant to indicate that Saleem, like Moses, never reaches the Promised Land—he dissolves before India has become what he wants it to become. Nevertheless, there is an ironic juxtaposition in that Saleem indicates hope that the country will eventually become a prosperous nation, whereas Sinai negates that same idea. Among Saleem's many parents, two other significant names are Mary Pereira and Joseph D'Costa, who show how Saleem might save his nation by sacrificing himself for it.

Shiva: Saleem's nemesis and alter ego bears the name of one of the major deities in the Hindu pantheon. Shiva takes on two opposite roles: On the one hand, he is the destroyer; on the other, the god of sensuality. In *Midnight's Children,* Shiva demonstrates his military prowess in the war against Pakistan and shows his sensual side in seducing apparently thousands of Indian women and having children by them (29/507). In many depictions, Shiva has a third eye, similar to the telepathic ability that connects him to Saleem and to the Midnight Children's Conference.

Tai: The boatman Tai is a tie to Kashmiri past and tradition, one that Aadam Aziz consciously breaks by introducing a bag of pigskin; however, the name lives on in the prostitute Tai Bibi, who can assume the smell of any human being.

Places

In addition to knowing about Indian history and Hindu mythology, it helps to know more about Indian geography to understand *Midnight's Children,* and not just because Saleem's face is like a map of India. As a microcosm of Indian history, religion, and politics, the importance of rural Kashmir, where the book begins and ends, has already been discussed. From Kashmir, Aadam moves his family to Agra, the home of the Taj Mahal, the most famous architectural icon of ancient India. Even though the Azizes do not spend much time there, the most recognizable of Indian monuments is another reminder of how intertwined are India and Great Britain. On the one hand, the structure was built in the seventeenth century by Shah Jahan for his wife, Mumtaz Mahal, an earlier jewel; at the same time, the building would not have survived if nineteenth-century British governor-general Lord Curzon had not taken interest and rescued it from dilapidation, a fact Rushdie points out in some of his nonfictional writing.

From Agra, the action in *Midnight's Children* moves to Bombay, and it is impossible to stress the importance of that city enough. It initially appears in the very first sentence of the novel. Early in his story, Saleem recalls an old rhyme about Bombay: "Prima in Indis/ Gateway to India/Star of the East/With her face to the West" (7/102) that summarizes what he feels: It is the foremost city of the Subcontinent both for its own population and for those arriving in India. It is also the most Western of all Indian cities, by which Rushdie means that it is cosmopolitan, multicultural, and tolerant. It is home to the Bombay film industry called Bollywood that outdoes Hollywood in its number of productions per year and supplies many metaphors for *Midnight's Children*. For Rushdie, who feels the same about the city as his protagonist, Bombay still remains home even though he has not lived there in a long time. He has said about *Midnight's Children* that "before I even knew the idea of the story, I had the idea of wanting to write about Bombay (Reder 18)." The city often changes its name—"Mumbadevi, Mumbabai, Mumbai" (7/ 101)—and it looks significantly different when Saleem arrives there with his son Aadam toward the end of his life. Saleem has difficulty comprehending the disappearance of the past, a literal as well as a metaphorical problem, but he is still "unable to resist uttering an ancient cry: 'Back-to-Bom!'" (30/520).

The story begins in Kashmir and Bombay, and ends in Bombay and Kashmir (with a detour via Delhi, which in *Midnight's Children* is mostly the city of politics with the Widow's presence and the ghetto of Communist magicians), but in between Saleem leaves India. His first stop (and second exile) is Pakistan, where he visits Rawalpindi and lives in Karachi. Saleem's life changes in Pakistan when his sinuses are drained, cutting his connection to the Midnight Children's Conference, but endowing him with a supernatural sense of smell. The only things he smells, however, are the negative aspects of economic class and religion: "I breathed in the fatalistic hopelessness of the slum dwellers and the smug defensiveness of the rich; I was sucked along the smell-trails of dispossession and also fanaticism" (22/352). Even the houses seem diseased here: "It was full of deformed houses . . . a wild proliferation of mad houses, whose inadequacies as living quarters were exceeded only by their quite exceptional ugliness" (22/354). For that reason, Saleem "never forgave Karachi for not being Bombay" (22/352).

Finally, Rushdie's protagonist visits the third country on the Subcontinent, Bangladesh, when he spends time in the Sundurbans during his tour as a military canine officer. (Stephens bases his deconstructionist interpretation on this episode.) This swamp on the border of India and Bangladesh at the Ganges delta is the largest mangrove forest in the world, and is inhabited by many wild animals, including crocodiles, tigers, and snakes—although the "blind, translucent serpent [that] bit, and poured venom into, [Saleem's] heel" (25/419) is an invention of Rushdie's. Rushdie, however, does not so much give a realistic description of a swamp as a phantasmagoric, dreamlike vision of a forest of horrors. Place correspondingly has a slightly different function than do urban settings: As Rushdie explains, within *Midnight's Children* as an epic, the Sundarban chapter allows him to perform a descent into hell (Reder 37). In the *Odyssey*, the protagonist sees the fallen heroes of the Trojan War as well as the seer Teiresias on his descent into hell; the entire first third of Dante's *Divine Comedy*, the *Inferno*, is one long descent where the author catalogs the sinners of his time. Saleem and his three companions similarly see apparitions that remind them of their own evil deeds and bear the physical consequences in paralysis or regression to childhood. In the end, however, the Sundurbans also allow the characters to come to terms with their past, or, in the Buddha's case, to rediscover it after years-long amnesia.

Literary Genre: The Novel

As the discussions of history, names, and places show, *Midnight's Children* is steeped in the cultures of India, from the specific events described to the allegorical meaning of the locations. It is already clear, however, that the East (an overly general and stereotypical term in the first place) is not the only influence. For instance, neither Aadam Aziz nor Saleem Sinai's names can be understood without reference to the Judeo-Christian tradition, and the descent into hell in the Sundurbans makes most sense in the Western literary form of the epic — or, more specifically, shows the overlap of Eastern and Western versions of epic. (Western epics include Homer's *Odyssey*, Virgil's *Aeneid*, and Milton's *Paradise Lost*; Eastern epics include the *Mahabarata* and the *Ramayana*.)

It is of even more importance that Rushdie writes in a distinctly Western literary genre, the novel. Although it is impossible to give a precise definition of that genre, it is safe to say that the novel developed in eighteenth-century Europe (mostly Britain) and integrated such earlier literary modes as Arthurian romance, spiritual autobiography, traditional epic, and news reporting. Perhaps the most salient feature of the genre was its novelty (i.e., the fact that it was *new*, or at least claimed to be). Even though a new genre might have developed from older forms at any point in time, there were three connected factors in the eighteenth century that are particularly significant for *Midnight's Children*: capitalism, colonialism, and racism. As an economic form, the novel relied on the new market of capitalism, where profit was the main motive for activity, where the individual was insignificant, and where a product had to be infinitely renewable to create continual financial turnover. Another aspect of this development was colonialism, which in economic terms meant the exploitation of colonies for the financial benefit of the home country, Great Britain (or Spain, or Portugal, or France, or Germany, or Belgium). Because of colonialism, the British began trading in India, and even though it took a long time for European administrative structures to compete with Indian government, cultural interchange started almost immediately. Finally, colonialism soon faced the ideological question of why it was acceptable to exploit the indigenous people of other countries, and the ingenious answer (from a colonialist point of view) was racism (i.e., the idea that other people, usually those with different skin pigmentation, were naturally inferior). It is too simple to see every form of capitalism, colonialism, and racism as purely evil because many Europeans probably genuinely believed that they were improving the lives of the people of South America, Africa, and Asia, but in terms of the impact on these peoples' lives there is not much good to be said. In India, the case was particularly interesting because racism played no role for the first hundred years of colonization—it only became prominent around the middle of the nineteenth century.

In any case, the eighteenth century was the time when such ideas as capitalism, colonialism, and racism developed, and it was the time when the literary form of the novel became one of the prime sites for the negotiation of these concepts. *Tristram Shandy*, by British writer Laurence Sterne, and published from 1759 to 1765, was one of the most significant novels of the eighteenth century. Arriving at a time when the genre was already pretty much established, *Tristram Shandy* took the usual novel plot of giving a young person's biography and leading up to their marriage (which was why most eighteenth-century novels simply had names as titles) and gave it a series of twists, several of which Rushdie copies in *Midnight's Children*. For instance, like Saleem, Tristram is not born until Volume III of the novel, but spends the first section describing the antics of his ancestors and relatives. Both novels are interested in scatology and sex (e.g., Saleem is as impotent as Tristrams's Uncle Toby), and the families of both protagonists are well known for their prominent noses. In addition, both *Tristram Shandy* and *Midnight's Children* are supposedly told to a female audience, in Sterne's case to Tristram's friend/listener/reader/companion Jenny, and in Rushdie's Saleem's wife Padma. Perhaps most importantly, both novels use a convoluted and digressive form of narration, constantly flashing back and forward, going off on tangents, and not finishing side stories. For that reason, *Tristram Shandy* is held up as the precursor of the postmodern novel (i.e., a form that employs lots of parody and irony, mixes different levels of culture, and rejects any kind of didactic mission for literature), whereas *Midnight's Children* is considered its contemporary paradigm.

It is more important that *Tristram Shandy*, coming as it did toward the end of the eighteenth century, challenged the ideological conventions of the Enlightenment. This is the main reason that Rushdie uses the novel as an intertext (i.e., another literary text that is frequently referred to for a specific purpose). In portraying a group of individuals mostly concerned with their own affairs, Sterne challenges capitalism, just as Rushdie throughout his novel criticizes such individuals as Major Zulfikar and his wife Emerald, who are mostly motivated by greed. The confrontation between competitive and cooperative economic models is staged particularly obviously in the Midnight Children's Conference, where Shiva advocates capitalism and Saleem some different form of interaction (i.e., not Communism, but a "third principle" [18/292, 294]). As both the eponymous hero and his Uncle Toby are fanatically interested in military history in *Tristram Shandy*, Sterne undermines such military enterprises as colonialism. Colonialism is obviously a presence (until 1947) and legacy (after 1947) in *Midnight's Children* that shapes Saleem's life as well as all of the nations on the Subcontinent. The British, however, are not the only power that is blamed here: West Pakistan has a colonial attitude toward East Pakistan in wanting to bring it into the "modern" age, and India has a paternal stance toward both, arrogating to itself the ability to help and advise when Bangladesh becomes an independent country. India also does not allow for Kashmiri independence, but forces the region to join it. In literary terms, colonialism was significant because the canon of British literature was to a large extent established in India, so Rushdie can challenge that by pointing back to its origins in the eighteenth century. For these reasons, his novel—and entire oeuvre—is frequently characterized as postcolonial.

Finally, as an outgrowth of colonialism, racism plays a larger role in *Midnight's Children* than is presented by *Tristram Shandy* because that novel mocks eighteenth-century theories of physiognomy that were the precursors of the racial theories of the nineteenth century. Hawes makes this argument in detail. In Rushdie's novel, Indians experience racism from the British as well as from each other: Early in the novel, the Reverend Mother even has a racist attitude toward her own daughter, "Mumtaz, the blackie whom she had never been able to love because of her skin of a South Indian fisherwoman" (4/58). Although this is clearly a critique of racism, Rushdie goes even further (following Sterne's lead) and dismantles the idea of basing quality and respect on pigmentation in his depiction of the Indian business community slowly becoming white as they emulate their British counterparts.

Literary Mode: Magic Realism

Even though Rushdie uses Sterne's *Tristram Shandy* to investigate the claims and ideologies of capitalism, colonialism, and racism, he uses a different text to look at the intersection between reality and fiction: Colombian author Gabriel García Márquez' *One Hundred Years of Solitude* (1967). This novel is particularly important because it counts as the seminal text of the literary mode known as magic realism.

The origins of magic realism go back to German expressionism and the post–World War II German novel; however, the term was subsequently mostly applied to South American fiction. Argentine author Jorge Luis Borges (1899–1988) was one of the foremost writers in the form, and Cuban Alejo Carpentier (1904–1980) contributed a significant theoretical reflection. At its most basic, *magic realism* is a mode of the literary genre novel that integrates magical events into an otherwise entirely realistic text. In *One Hundred Years of Solitude*, for instance, a character suddenly drifts off toward the sky while she is hanging laundry. It is of note that none of the other characters in the novel display any surprise at this event, so *within* the book even flying is entirely realistic. In other words, magic realism makes what in *our* world is magic into realism within the *fictional* world.

There are many magic realist elements in *Midnight's Children*. As is typical in magic realism, some of these are incorporated from fairy tales, folk tales, and traditional myths—with the difference that here they are taken as completely normal. For instance, at the beginning of the novel, the boatman Tai tells the young Aadam Aziz that he is hundreds or thousands of years old—"I have watched the mountains being born; I have seen Emperors die. . . . I saw that Isa, that Christ, when he came to Kashmir" (1/11)—and nobody objects. Toward the end of the book, the boatman's namesake, the prostitute Tai Bibi, "possessed a mastery over her glands so total that she could alter her bodily odors to match those of anyone on earth" (22/365), which makes her irresistible to Saleem. Throughout *Midnight's Children*, various cooks put their emotions into food with specific emotional and physical results, a magic realist trope well known from Mexican writer Laura Esquivel's novel and film, *Like Water for Chocolate*. The fading of Ahmed Sinai can similarly only be explained by magical means: "Gradually his skin paled, his hair lost its color, until within a few months he had become entire white" (12/204). His testicles turn into ice cubes because his financial assets are frozen, but his wife does not seem to find that strange (9/154). There is a difference between Rushdie's and South American magic realism, however, in that the elements in *Midnight's Children* are not always accepted by the other characters in the novel: It is unclear if anyone else knows of Tai Bibi's power, and only the narrator Saleem appears to be aware of the psychological and physical impact of meals. In an even more complicated fashion, the same is true of Saleem's death, dissolving into 600 million particles (30/533). As a device, it would be straightforward magic realism; however, only he knows about his condition, and doctors who diagnose him actually specifically deny it; in addition, it remains uncertain at the very end of the novel what fate Saleem meets.

The most important magic realist element in Rushdie's novel, however, is the Midnight Children's Conference. Constituted of the 581 surviving of the 1001 children born between midnight and one o'clock in the morning on the day of Independence, August 15, 1947, all members have supernatural powers. (The larger number refers to the *Arabian Nights*, where Scheherazade has to tell stories for 1001 nights to stop King Shahryar from killing her, and which are almost as unreal; 581 is the number of members in the Indian parliament. Thus, once again, Rushdie integrates a "Western" form because García Marquez is considered part of the Western tradition, and such "Eastern" culture as Arab literature and Indian politics.) Earlier, Saleem has discovered his own telepathic abilities and has been slapped half deaf as a reward for telling his family (11/187). On his tenth birthday, due to an accident where he hits his head, Saleem discovers the ability to communicate with the other 580 children. He learns that other Midnight's Children can step through mirrors, multiply fish, turn into werewolves, change their size, transform from man into woman, inflict wounds with words, eat metal, fly higher than a bird, and so on (14/227f.) The closer to midnight the children are born, the stronger are their powers. Saleem, his opponent Shiva, and his friend Parvati are born closest to midnight and are the only ones of the Midnight's Children who are fully developed as characters within the novel. Still, more important than the mere presence of magic realism is the question of its meaning or significance. Saleem, or Rushdie, addresses the problem himself—and at the reader—within *Midnight's Children*:

Reality can have metaphorical content; that does not make it less real. A thousand and one children were born; there were a thousand and one possibilities which had never been present in one place at one time before; and there were a thousand and one dead ends. Midnight's children can be made to represent many things, according to your point of view; they can be seen as the last throw of everything antiquated and retrogressive in our myth-ridden nation, whose defeat was entirely desirable in the context of modernizing, twentieth-century economy; or as the true hope of freedom, which is now forever extinguished; but what they must not become is the bizarre creation of a rambling, diseased mind (14/230).

In true magic realist fashion, Saleem insists that the people and events he describes are true, however difficult they are to believe. He also points to the familiar origins of magic realist elements in myth (i.e., leaving out such literary precedents as *One Hundred Years of Solitude* [flying], the *Bible* [multiplying fish], *Alice in Wonderland* [changing size], or Rushdie's own earlier novel *Grimus* [changing gender]). In this sense, the Midnight's Children are an acknowledgment of the Indian tradition of oral entertainment. It is of more importance that Saleem raises the possibility that the Midnight's Children mean hope, or represent the past. In the latter reading, it is good and perhaps unavoidable that they are exterminated because they have no place in the twentieth century; however, Rushdie probably approves more of the first interpretation, according to which the Midnight's Children stand for the many possibilities that India had after Independence. Rushdie similarly uses the Midnight's Children to create a new pluralist and secular version of India on an allegorical level. Every one of the 1001 children has a particular vision of the country (e.g., one where gender no longer matters, one where industrialism is present but under control, one where humans and nature coexist peacefully, one where transportation is no problem), but 420 have already been destroyed by Saleem's tenth birthday, and by the end of the book all are dead or impotent. In addition, as Brennan argues, even though most magic realism is a way to subvert colonialist discourse, it is only a temporary release from repression in *Midnight's Children*: Britain's colonialism is soon replaced by Indira Gandhi's Emergency.

Beyond that, however, the Midnight's Children symbolize a part of the relationship between reality and fiction. For Rushdie, reality is not simply the hard facts visible in the world; rather, it is also the "metaphorical content" that can be found there (i.e., the ideas, thoughts, concepts, theories, programs, hopes, and dreams that human beings have). At a different point in *Midnight's Children*, Saleem already tries to dissect the relationship between his life and the nation—which might as well be fiction and reality—but he only comes up with a schematic series of adjectives ("actively–literally, passively–metaphorically, actively–metaphorically, and passively–literally, I was inextricably intertwined with my world" [17/272f.]); now, he is more sophisticated and less doctrinal about it. Rushdie makes use here of a different meaning of the term *magic realism*. According to some critics, the reason this mode of literature developed in interwar Germany and later continued in postwar South America is that in those places in particular it was difficult for authors to reconcile the reality in which they were living with the world they *wanted* to inhabit. Political and historical events (e.g., military government and sky-high inflation) seemed so ludicrous that there was little point in trying to stick to "reality" any longer. In Rushdie's own words, García Márquez perceived a "reality-gulf in Latin America: an unbridgeable gulf between the view of the world prevalent in his Colombian village and the one that held sway in the cities; a gulf, too, between the truth and its manipulated, official versions" ("Indian Writer" 81f.). The "real" history of India that Rushdie saw in the first thirty years of his and the nation's life was similarly so fantastical that a traditional realist novel could not properly describe it. By using magic realism as popularized by Gabriel García Márquez, he was able to represent a different, but internally consistent, version of reality that met the needs of his novel to offer alternative visions of India.

Literary Voice: Nationalism

With the eighteenth-century novel, Rushdie was able to interrogate such concepts as capitalism, colonialism, and racism; with magic realism, he found a device to create a real-yet-not-real world in which he could explore alternative Indias. These two come together in the novel that is the most important intertext for *Midnight's Children*, the novel *The Tin Drum* (1959) by German Nobel Prize winner Günter Grass. Rushdie has subsequently acknowledged his debt to Sterne and García Márquez, but his connection to Grass is closest, as is documented by various laudatory comments of one about the other, including a preface Rushdie wrote to a collection of Grass' essays and a conversation between the two.

The Tin Drum, like *Midnight's Children*, is told by a physically unusual narrator. Whereas Saleem is notable for his huge nose,

missing digit, and spotty hair, Oskar Matzerath decides to stop growing at the age of three and remains that size for the rest of his life.
Like *Midnight's Children*, *The Tin Drum* does not start with Oskar's
life, but rather with the story of his grandparents. Both novels are
narrated in the present under stressful circumstances: Saleem, of
course, is falling apart; Oskar is locked up in a mental ward. The
locations for the two books are two of the more cosmopolitan and
multicultural cities of their areas (i.e., Bombay for Rushdie and Ger-
man-Polish-Russian Gdansk for Grass), which are the authors' home
towns. They follow their (anti)heroes through war and migration to
new homes in different countries. Both stories take place in times of
national upheaval: *Midnight's Children* is set first during the movement for independence, then during the time of the new nation of
India; *The Tin Drum* begins at the turn of the nineteenth to the
twentieth century, and follows Germany through two world wars,
ending in the new (West) German republic after 1945. To some extent, both authors assess the development of their new countries and
find it wanting because of historical amnesia. In addition, both novels expose and criticize the susceptibility of the bourgeoisie to au-
thoritarianism.

Of course, these parallels are no more than amusing literary de-
tective work as long as they do not add to the understanding of *Midnight's Children*. Knowledge of *The Tin Drum*, however, can indeed
contribute to the interpretation of Rushdie's novel because it draws
further attention to the question of the nation and nationalism.
Throughout Grass' work, there is little doubt that most forms of pa-
triotism are highly suspect. For one thing, Gdansk belongs to different nations in the course of history, so it is impossible even to figure
out to whom to be loyal. In *Midnight's Children*, Saleem's loyalties
are similarly divided as he moves (in the story, if not his own life)
from British colony to India and Pakistan to Bangladesh. It is never
clear what really makes each nation distinct, and why there should

be any emotional connection between the individual and his or her place of residence. Right after Independence, Saleem is particularly direct about the status of his nation (although the thoughts probably apply to any other country as well):

A nation which had never previously existed [India] was about to win its freedom, catapulting us into a world which, although it had five thousand years of history, although it had invented the game of chess and traded with Middle Kingdom Egypt, was nevertheless quite imaginary; into a mythical land, a country which would never exist except by the efforts of a phenomenal collective will—except in a dream we all agreed to dream; it was a mass fantasy shared in varying degrees by Bengali and Punjabi, Madrasi and Jat, and would periodically need the sanctification and renewal which can only be provided by rituals of blood. India, the new myth—a collective fiction in which anything was possible (8/124f).

Like post–World War II Germany, India is a country that has a long tradition, but is new as a political entity, so nationalism cannot be based on cultural or economic achievements. Instead, the nation takes on the status of myth, which is usually associated with stories or events in the distant past. This myth is unreal in the sense that it is like a dream, but it is real in that many individuals have come together and made a conscious choice to participate in the project. Saleem and Rushdie are painfully aware of the limitations of the idea (i.e., it will require human sacrifices, it is not shared in exactly the same way by every citizen, and the dreamers better not wake up), but also apparently admire the audacity of the concept. The country India is a "phenomenal" idea, and if developed properly, might have any kind of outcome. Of course, by the end of *Midnight's Children* it is clear that most of the options have been shut down, and despair has set in after the neologistic operation of "sperectomy: the draining-out of hope" (29/503) performed on the Midnight's Children, who, after all, represent the possibilities of India. Still, *nation* is a powerful idea and should not be discounted, if only because of the actions it inspires.

East, West

The analysis of the historical, cultural, geographical, and literary background of *Midnight's Children* already reveals many of the themes in the novel (e.g., Indian history, East and West, the importance of names and places, identity, gender, literary tradition, capitalism, colonialism, racism, nationalism, history, and reality). The mere recognition of these themes, however, is not sufficient. The question remains: What does *Midnight's Children* actually *say* about these issues?

Rushdie clearly incorporates many ideas that are typically considered "Eastern" or "Western" into *Midnight's Children*. For example, the setting in India, Pakistan, and Bangladesh is Eastern, as are many of the names from Hindu mythology. Furthermore, the idea of *maya* or illusion is Hindu; the mundane and horrible are juxtaposed in the battlefield scene after the Sundurbans in a way that could be interpreted as Eastern; and the principle of the permeable body is Ayurvedic. On the other side, the literary genre of the novel that Rushdie chooses is Western, as are other names from the Judeo-Christian tradition. Some of the characters can be interpreted as embodiments of Kashmiri (Tai) or Muslim (Naseem) ideas and virtues, whereas others consciously bring economic (Ahmed) or technological (Aadam) innovations into their culture. In the novel as a whole, however, there is no clear assessment of any of these ideas or tendencies. On the one hand, both Aadam Aziz and Ahmed Sinai fail in their modernization projects; on the other, Tai dies a futile death and Naseem retreats to her role as Reverend Mother. The British as colonizers are mostly criticized as hypocritical and false—

even Methwold's immaculate hair ultimately proves to be a wig—
but then again Indian politicians are unable to give the country a
powerful and successful new direction, too. If anything, those who
mostly adhere closely to what they consider a "pure" tradition are
most likely to fail, and are most strongly criticized. Pakistan, for example, which (wrongly) believes its name to mean, "Land of the
Pure," is the place where Saleem loses his ability to communicate
telepathically with the other Midnight's Children.

With the juxtaposition of "East" and "West," then, Rushdie
seems to be making a statement on at least two levels. First of all,
neither East nor West have better ideas, possess a stronger heritage,
or should be valued over the other. In his personal history, Saleem
represents a mix of Britain and India: For his first ten years he believes himself to be the child of Indian parents, then he realizes that
the Sinais are not his real parents; however, he ultimately learns that
his biological parents are probably Vanita Winkie and William
Methwold. In other words, he is a hybrid between East and West.
The same is true for both his genealogical heritage and for his cultural upbringing: He is raised in an Indian family, but one where
the grandfather has studied in Germany and where the father has
both bought a British estate and has taken on the habits and rituals
of its previous owners. Because Saleem is the "hero" of *Midnight's
Children*, it can be surmised that Rushdie believes this mix of cultures to be a good thing. Beyond the mix of "East" and "West," however, it is important to recognize on a second level that these
categories are constantly subverted and undermined in *Midnight's
Children*. For one thing, neither East nor West are as homogeneous
as the terms would make them seem to be: India is only one part of
the East, and is torn internally between many, many groups; Britain,
to some extent, stands for the West, but is different from the United
States as represented by Evie Burns or Portugal symbolized by
Mary's Goan last name Pereira and the name of her Braganza pickle

factory, taken from the "poor Queen Catharine [of Braganza, Portuguese princess and later British queen] who gave these islands to the British" (30/528). For these reasons, *Midnight's Children* can be partly interpreted as a confrontation between East and West where neither comes off too well, but, more importantly, the novel demonstrates that those categories in themselves are often not very useful.

Allegory

The idea that concepts generally believed to be complete and pure are really fragmented and contentious extends to many other theories in the book (e.g., nation, culture, gender, and identity). As described earlier, the biography of Saleem in *Midnight's Children* runs parallel to the history of the nation of India. For that reason, many critics take the novel to be a national allegory for Indian history. This interpretation is promoted within the novel when William Methwold speaks of the "very Indian lust for allegory" (7/106). An allegory is a story that has two levels of meaning, an explicit, literal meaning, and an implicit, allegorical meaning. For instance, in the most famous allegory of English literature, Paul Bunyan's *Pilgrim's Progress* (1678–84), the protagonist Christian — on the literal level — finds out that his home town is about to be destroyed by fire and travels through a series of places such as the Slough of Despond, the Valley of Humiliation, and Vanity Fair until he reaches his new home in Celestial City. His companions along the way include people with names like Worldly Wiseman, Faithful, and Hopeful. On the allegorical level, of course, this is a description of the devoted Christian's journey through life's challenges, accompanied by other human beings who either help him along his way or draw him toward hell, to ultimate salvation and arrival in heaven.

According to this model, Saleem's life in *Midnight's Children* is an allegory for the development of India. For instance, his birth stands for the birth of India, and his growing pains represent the growing pains of his country. For this reason, Nehru's letter to Saleem (which adds plenty of pressure to the young child's life) says, "We shall be watching your life with the closest attention; it will be, in a sense, the mirror of our own" (9/139). Saleem's move to all three countries on the Subcontinent in the course of his life symbolizes how those nations at different points in time are most important in the development of the region, and Saleem's own happiness or unhappiness in his various homes shows how those places promote more or less savory policies. The failure of the Midnight Children's Conference (with its 581 members an allegorical reminder of Indian parliament) parallels the failure of India to live up to its promise as a nation, and Saleem's disintegration at the end of the book—on Independence Day (30/532)—demonstrates that India is falling apart.

The allegorical reading of *Midnight's Children*, however, is not entirely satisfactory for several reasons, and not just because Rushdie has said that "one of the problems is that [in Indian criticism] there's an expectation of allegory which is so great that almost everything you do is translated allegorically. I don't think that anything I've done can be translated in that simple way" (Reder 63), and that, "I didn't want to write a book which could be conventionally translated as allegory" (*Midnight's Children* 3). Above all, allegory does not usually contain the historical characters and events that are so prominent in Rushdie's novel. It is difficult to sustain this kind of interpretation when the literal and allegorical levels are already mixed in the book itself. Second, allegories tend to be simplistic, and it is certainly misleading to consider *Midnight's Children* an easy novel. For Bunyan in the seventeenth century, both the world and his faith were perfectly clear, and he had no problem constructing a one-to-one correspondence between the two; for Rushdie in the twentieth, this kind of clarity is no longer a good way to understand and represent the world. Finally, there are just too many details in the book that do not fit into an allegorical interpretation. In this analysis, it is difficult, if not impossible, to account for such characters as Naseem, Mumtaz, or Jamila, such situations as the leveling of the magicians' quarter, and such narrative devices as Padma's presence or Saleem's self-reflection. Nevertheless, there is obviously truth to the allegorical reading in that *Midnight's Children* definitely criticizes the development of India after Independence for not fulfilling the economic hopes of its citizens, for continuing to foster religious violence, and. more specifically, for Indira Gandhi's Emergency.

Nation

Once again, however, Rushdie's fictional analysis goes beyond the particular and into a more philosophical realm. He levels strong accusations at India, but India is only one country that plays a role in *Midnight's Children*: There are also Pakistan, Bangladesh, and Great Britain, to name the most obvious ones. More than just criticizing a particular country or government, then, Rushdie has a problem with the idea of the nation state in general.

As the quote presented earlier shows, Rushdie sees India as a country based on an imaginative leap. Even though nation states are built in theory on some coherence between their members (i.e., ethnicity, religion, language, at least a common contract or goal) India has no unifying concept. Kashmiris, Punjabis, Bombayites, and Calcuttans have very little in common with regard to culture or history; Muslims, Hindus, Sikhs, and Christians barely get along despite the supposedly pacific bent of some of their religions; speakers of Hindi, Urdu, Marathi, Bengali, and Malayam cannot communicate except in the colonizers' English language; the traditional division of Indian society by caste has to be overcome; residents of the Subcontinent have no choice in which country to live, with disastrous results during Partition and even later in places like Kashmir. These fragmenting tendencies appear again and again in fictional form in *Midnight's Children*. To complicate the issue even more, the countries on the Subcontinent are not even divided by their own leaders, but by the departing British administration. In addition, the countries that *do* seem to have a coherent idea or mission (e.g., Pakistan as a Muslim state) either make a hash of that mission or idea, or live up to it only by violently suppressing those who disagree. In *Midnight's Children*, General Zulfikar and his wife, Emerald, are more pure in their monetary greed than in their Islamic beliefs, and the country leads what amounts to a civil war when its Eastern section does not want to live the same way. Rushdie suggests that Great Britain is similarly held together mostly by its imperial enterprise, and such colonial administrators as William Methwold fall apart when they have to return to England.

It is difficult, however, to find an alternative to these faulty and repressive ideas of nationhood in *Midnight's Children*. Democracy in itself is clearly not much help because a ruler such as Indira Gandhi can subvert the democratic process with populist propaganda or simply suspend it with the Emergency when it serves her purposes. Other democratic countries, such as the United States, are mentioned, but they do not get enough space to become models. Constitutional monarchy in the British version is no alternative either, nor is the straightforward monarchy of pre–World War I Germany where Aadam Aziz studies, and which is already being undermined by radicals. The main Cold War alternative to democracy, socialism (or communism in terms of ideology rather than form of government), is important in the Indian context and gets some respect (in spite of what Booker argues in *"Midnight's Children*, History, and Complexity"), but ultimately fails as well. Early in Saleem's life, Nadir Khan in his new incarnation as Qasim the Red, "official candidate of the official Communist Party of India" (15/248), makes some electoral headway, but is squashed by the goons of the Congress Party; later the inhabitants of the ghetto of the magicians, who "were Communists, almost to a man" (27/457), bicker too much among themselves to be politically effective, and, in the end, are more literally squashed by Sanjay Gandhi's program to remove the slums of Delhi.

The only real alternative that Rushdie offers as a model for the political structure and goals of a nation state is the Midnight Children's Conference. Here, individuals with a wide variety of ideas and capabilities come together with not much more purpose than communication. Rushdie even indicates the cerebral quality of this exchange of ideas by making it entirely telepathic. In the first conversation between Saleem and Shiva, the latter wants the Conference simply to serve *him*, whereas Saleem envisions a more cooperative endeavor: "The thing is, we must be here for a *purpose*, don't you think? I mean, there has to be a *reason*, you must agree? So what I thought, we should try and work out what it is, and then, you know, sort of dedicate our lives to . . ." (15/252; Rushdie's ellipsis). Although "reason" suggests something that is already present and that the Midnight's Children only need to discover, "purpose" indicates that they must invent and implement their mission. In addition, in the hesitant punctuation, the incomplete sentences, and the question, Rushdie indicates that this alternative politics, which he also calls the "third principle" (18/292), is more of an idea than a program—a "try" rather than a success. At one point, Saleem defines the "third principle": "its name is childhood. But it dies; or rather, it is murdered" (18/294). For a while, the members of the Conference do work together and discuss their purpose, with possibilities ranging from collectivism to individualism, filial duty to infant revolution, capitalism to altruism, science to religion, and courage to cowardice (16/261), but they are ultimately unable to come to an agreement. One member even foresees the Conference's demise long before Indira Gandhi's sterilization program (16/262), but at least for a few pages in *Midnight's Children* there is some hope for a nation that is built on the peaceful coexistence of many varying ideas rather than the imposition of one particular model. In a nutshell, the idea is: "There are as many versions of India as Indians" (19/308). Rushdie rejects pretty much every available political philosophy and form of government and in their place installs the utopia of harmonious multitudes. In other words, both in his discussion of East and West and in his analysis of the nation state, Rushdie condemns most of the ideas available, and he denounces the very concepts as confusing and counterproductive.

Identity

For Rushdie, this harmonious multitude that might form a different kind of nation is not just characteristic of states, but also of individuals. From the very beginning of *Midnight's Children*, Saleem insists, "Please believe that I am falling apart" (3/36), and for most of the novel he fights his impending demise. Toward the end of the book, however, he realizes not only that his doom is inevitable, but also that he should embrace his new situation.

Saleem's falling apart is of course on the one hand a magic realist device that allegorically represents the disintegration of India. It is just as important, however, that it symbolizes Saleem's *identity* breaking into pieces—he no longer knows who he is. As discussed earlier, at the beginning of his life, he believes that he is the son of Ahmed and Amina Sinai; later he thinks his parents are Wee Willie Winkie and Vanita, only to realize that Vanita cheated on her husband with William Methwold. Finally Saleem picks for himself a series of mothers and fathers, the latter including the European doctor Schaapsteker (who saves his life), Nadir Khan (who takes him under his wings), his uncle Hanif (who introduces him to the cinema), his other uncle Zulfikar (who teaches him politics), and finally Picture Singh (who helps rescue him from Bangladesh and start life anew in India). To some extent, this confusion about heritage speaks to the cultural mix of India and in Saleem, but, just as importantly, it addresses the fact that personal identity is never as clear and complete as the individual would like. At the extreme, Saleem realizes that everybody in the world contributes to his identity, and that he has ingested the whole world to become who he is: "I have been a swallower of lives; and to know me, just the one of me, you'll have to swallow the lot as well. Consumed multitudes are jostling and shoving inside me" (1/4). The choice of language here shows that for Rushdie, identity is constructed in two directions: Saleem is victim of his background, but he also "swallows" the lives around him. The formulation "one of me" indicates that there is really *more* than one Saleem, which could mean that there is more than one aspect to his identity, or at the very least that he changes so much over his life that he is no longer the same person. That is a frightening thought because it rejects a concrete and unified notion of the self, but it is also a liberating one because it allows for what contemporary critics call self-fashioning independent of familial, historical, or cultural influences. Finally, the passage suggests that the lives that are swallowed are not passive, but fight back to tell *their* stories. In other words, Saleem's identity is fluid, and is constantly challenged by everyone around him. These sentiments are summarized in a remarkable passage after Saleem has gone through the experience of losing his identity entirely through amnesia, but has recently regained his memory. Here, he is not even certain if he is a person or a thing, and mixes being an actor and a victim, present and past. Finally, he clarifies that his condition is not particularly unusual, but is instead simply typical for all human beings:

Who what am I? My answer: I am the sum total of everything that went before me, of all that I have seen, of everything done-to-me. I am everyone everything whose being-in-the-world affected was affected by mine. I am anything that happens after I've gone which would not have happened if I had not come. Nor am I particularly exceptional in this matter; each "I," every one of the now-six-hundred-million-plus of us, contains a similar multitude. I repeat for the last time: To understand me, you'll have to swallow the world (26/440f.).

Rushdie himself is one of the multitudes whom Saleem swallows, and who swallows him in return. In terms of his own identity, Rushdie has often used the term *hybrid*—he is made up of several parts. He is most obviously Indian as well as English; at the same time, he is specifically an Indian Muslim, although in the cultural more than in the religious sense, his family no longer lives in India but in Pakistan, and he himself has moved on from London to New York. In the title essay of the first volume of his collected essays, *Imaginary Homelands*, Rushdie argues that it constitutes a strength rather than a weakness to be part of this "culture and political history of the phenomenon of migration, displacement, life in a minority group" (20). He believes that—as for Saleem—"it is perhaps one of the more pleasant freedoms of the literary migrant to be able to choose his parents" (20f.). Furthermore, this condition is not exceptional, but typical for almost any individual in the contemporary world. Rushdie even forces his readers in *Midnight's Children* to take the role of the migrants by placing them in position of the Other and by the frequent interruptions in the text. Thus, Rushdie becomes a spokesman for cultural displacement and for a positive evaluation of the experience of migrancy.

Women and Narration

Identity is particularly fluid, it seems, for the women around Saleem. This shows most obviously in their constantly changing names, (which do not make the novel any easier to follow): Naseem Aziz becomes the Reverend Mother, Mumtaz turns into Amina, Parvati is renamed Laylah, and the Brass Monkey becomes Jamila Singer. The only woman who seems to have a stable identity is Saleem's interlocutor, Padma, but then she lacks much background in terms of family, social class, or even geography, so her identity is only stable in the sense of not being there at all. On the other hand, this absence of identity makes sense in terms of the narrative setup of *Midnight's Children*: Padma is the *tabula rasa* or blank slate on whom Saleem writes his history. She must be ignorant both of his stories and of herself to be able to serve as a vessel for his biography.

It could be argued that Padma is too naïve to serve as the surrogate for the reader in *Midnight's Children*: Readers need to be smarter than her to pick up on the intertextual references to other literature that Rushdie scatters throughout his text. Yet Padma is also paradigmatic as the silenced female who willingly acquiesces to her subjugation and is absent from such key moments of the narrative as the beginning of the story in Chapter 1 or the sterilization of the Midnight's Children in Chapter 29. This suggests that Rushdie might be a sexist author. It is indeed possible to discern a streak of misogyny in *Midnight's Children*, from the popularity of marital infidelity in females to the exaggerated figure of the Widow and Saleem's practical servitude to the various women in his life; however, it would be too easy to ascribe this antifeminism to Rushdie, who is, after all, not the same as Saleem—the reader could just as well be meant to criticize Saleem for his position on women. Furthermore, Padma ultimately "wins" over Saleem by convincing him to marry her. In practical narrative terms, Padma's intelligence and her independence do not really matter anyway because she is merely the audience for Saleem. That does not mean that she does not participate: Her insistence that Saleem not digress too much is what makes the novel *Midnight's Children* possible. It also does not mean that

Padma is not important: She is Saleem's "necessary ear" (11/170), and when she storms out because he has exasperated her, the story grinds to a halt.

By creating Padma the way he does—with "ignorance and super-stition, necessary counterweights to my miracle-laden omni-science," and a "paradoxical earthiness of spirit" (11/170)—Rushdie makes a statement about narrative theory (i.e., the way he believes that story-telling and literature work). In interviews about *Midnight's Children*, he has stressed that "Padma enabled the book to become an oral narrative" (Reder 14), which he considers a particularly In-dian form of literature. Thus, the character Padma allows Rushdie to do two things: to introduce another specifically "Eastern" aspect (oral narration) into his novel, this time into the specifically "West-ern" literary genre of the novel; and to make it crystal-clear that for him, literature is not something that is created as a finished, self-enclosed artifact by an author and that readers simply have to accept in the form it is presented. For Rushdie, literature is a co-operation between author and audience, between reader and writer, which also explains why Saleem is as chatty with his audience as he is. As early as the first paragraph of the novel, his comment, "Oh, spell it out, spell it out" (1/3, repeated on several occasions later in the novel, such as 21/348 and 28/482) must be construed as a response either to a direct question from the as-yet-unnamed listener, or as an anticipation to an objection that a reader might raise. At the very end of *Midnight's Children*, Saleem's comment, "No, that won't do" (30/532), about his own story similarly must be a reaction to his ac-tual or imagined readership, and his series of rhetorical questions on how to end the novel (30/531) must be addressed to someone. This relation between reader and writer is not just important as a narrative device, however, but also because it forces the readers to be involved actively in the content and message (i.e., forces them to participate in the message that Rushdie is trying to convey).

Style

Throughout *Midnight's Children*, one of Saleem's and Rushdie's concerns is to make the story coherent. Because East and West, India, and even individuals' identities are constantly falling apart and fragmenting into millions of pieces, there has to be something that keeps the story together. Saleem mentions this desire to keep things together in reverse at the very beginning of the novel, when he says, "I admit it: above all things, I fear absurdity" (1/4), and he partly explains it as "a sort of national longing for form" (21/344). At the same time, he recognizes that coherence cannot be avoided: "There is no escape from form" (16/259). This is confirmed at the end of the novel, where Saleem notices, "Form—once again, recurrence and shape!—no escape from it" (29/506). To some extent, Rushdie achieves the effect of unity through his reader, who is impersonated in Padma. As a specific audience, Padma is annoying to Saleem because she insists on a chronologically linear narrative (i.e., she always wants to know what happens next [3/37]); however, Rushdie stylistically attempts to make his story consistent through leitmotifs (i.e., through images that recur throughout the novel and remind the reader of previous situations). Rushdie even mentions this device himself (*Midnight's Children* 3f.). For instance, the sheet is an important leitmotif. Early in the story, Aadam Aziz meets his future wife, Naseem Ghani, when he, as a doctor, is called to treat her. Because Naseem lives in purdah, which means that she cannot be seen by a male other than her father, she exposes only the actually or supposedly sick parts of her body to her doctor—through a hole in a sheet. This method of presentation has a metaphorical as well as a literal meaning: Aadam, who after his stint in Germany is trying to comprehend India again, can do so only in fragments, and Naseem's personality is made up of bits and pieces that he has to put together from what he sees. The thing that makes the sheet a leitmotif, however, is that it reappears at key moments later in the story; for example, when it is accidentally used as a ghost costume by the third generation of Aziz/Sinai children (2/28).

Another leitmotif is the snake or serpent. In one form, this appears in the game of snakes and ladders, which even gets its own chapter title (10/155). Early in his life, Saleem "fell in love with Snakes and Ladders. O perfect balance of rewards and penalties! O seemingly random choices made by tumbling dice!" (10/160). In rapturous language, he extols the virtues of this board game, emphasizing that it represents the dualities of the world (e.g., East and West, good and bad, up and down) more perfectly than any other game. He soon realizes, unfortunately, "that the game lacked one crucial dimension, that of ambiguity—because, as events are about to show, it is also possible to slither down a ladder and climb to triumph on the venom of a snake" (10/161). As discussed earlier, Rushdie does not believe that dichotomies or mutually exclusive opposites are very helpful in understanding the world, and the game of snakes and ladders allows him to show this to his young protagonist.

In addition to the board game, however, snakes appear at several key points in the narrative. First, when Saleem falls ill as a baby, no doctor can help him. Finally, the family's neighbor, Doctor Schaapsteker (a name that sounds as if it meant "sharp sting")—who acts like a snake himself with his "tongue flicking at the corners of his mouth" (10/169)—rescues him with "[d]iluted venene of the king cobra" (ibid.). But Schaapsteker, now considered one of Saleem's fathers, also points out that the venom can kill as well as save lives. Analyzing his own last name, Saleem points out that "Sin is also the letter S, as sinuous as a snake" (21/348). Later in *Midnight's Children*, a snake again plays a significant role when "a blind, translucent serpent" (25/419) bites Saleem and restores his memory. Whereas the image of another snake helps bind this passage to the rest of the novel, the fact that it is transparent distinguishes it, perhaps symbolizing Saleem's completely empty state of his mind at the time. Other snakes include the ones that Picture Singh, "the Most Charming Man In The World" (26/435), enchants with his flute, as well as the "Serpent" (10/162) who assassinates Mahatma Gandhi. Of course, any form of snake is associated in the Judeo-Christian context with Satan, who comes to seduce Eve in the shape of a serpent, but Rushdie is more ambivalent and makes it very clear that nothing is ever entirely good or bad.

History

With the snake bite in the Sundurbans, Saleem's memories come rushing back, but even during his ordeal in the jungle he has held on to another object that functions as a leitmotif: the silver spittoon. This vessel comes into the possession of the Aziz/Sinai family as a wedding gift from the Rani of Cooch Naheen to Mumtaz and Nadir Khan (4/61) and follows them throughout their travels across the Subcontinent. Toward the end of his story, when the magicians' ghetto in Delhi is being razed, Saleem thinks of two things: his son and his spittoon (29/495). Whereas Aadam is rescued, the spittoon finally meets its end under Sanjay Gandhi's bulldozers. In between, it has its most significant moment (and is almost endowed with a personality) when Saleem is felled by a bomb falling on Karachi:

. . . now something which has hidden unseen for many years is circling in the night like a whirligig piece of the moon, something catching the light of the moon and falling now falling as I pick myself up dizzily after the blast, something twisting turning somersaulting down, silver as the moonlight, a wondrously worked silver spittoon inlaid with lapis lazuli, the past plummeting towards me like a vulture-dropped hand to become what-purifies-and-sets-me-free (23/392).

In this typically breathless passage, which is part of a two-page tor-rential sentence summarizing Saleem's memories (391–93), adjec-tives are strung together without commas, whereas commas replace the periods between what should be separate sentences to reproduce the sense of anxiety and bewilderment that the character feels. The spittoon is equated with Saleem himself, who after all is known as "Piece-of-the-Moon" (1/3). He finally achieves the purity that Paki-stan is supposed to represent, but not in the way the country's found-ers intended: He is wiped clean of his past and memory, almost like Padma in other parts of the book. This allows Rushdie to reflect on one of the most important subjects of the book—history.

For Rushdie, history is important because it connects people to their past, making them more well-rounded (if never complete) human beings. History is constructed through memory, and once Saleem loses his memory, he is severed from his past and becomes no more than an animal, serving on the CUTIA as a dog. In that unit, his fellow soldiers try to find out his background, but Saleem responds, "Don't try and fill my head with history. I am who I am, that's all there is to it" (24/403). Here, Rushdie is indicating that on the contrary, humans are *not* simply who they are, but are indeed an accumulation of their history. Saleem cannot recognize this fact because of his amnesia, but much too much has happened at this point in *Midnight's Children* for the reader to accept that the past does not matter.

At the same time, Rushdie believes in a certain *form* of history, which again he can address mostly through the device of the spit-toon, but also through another leitmotif, the pickle. Saleem, of course, tells his story from Mary Pereira's Braganza pickle factory, where he as well as Padma work, and he compares the "mastery of the multiple gifts of cookery and language" (3/37) to each other—he can be a writer and make chutneys at the same time. As a matter of fact, the two activities are quite similar, he explains: ". . . by day amongst the pickle-vats, by night within these sheets, I spend my time at the great work of preserving. Memory, as well as fruit, is being saved from the corruption of the clocks" (ibid.). Later, the chapters are even described as pickle-jars: At the beginning of Chapter 26, Saleem writes, "Twenty-six pickle-jars stand gravely on a shelf; twenty-six special blends, each with its identifying label, neatly inscribed with familiar phrases: 'Movements Performed by Pepperpots,' for instance, or 'Alpha and Omega,' or 'Commander Sabarmati's Baton'" (27/442)—the titles of Chapters 20, 16, and 18, respectively. The final chapter of *Midnight's Children* is similarly described as "Special Formula No. 30: 'Abracadabra'" (30/529), and Saleem concludes that "in words and pickles, I have immortalized by memories" (ibid.).

This process, which he also calls "the chutnification of history" (ibid.), finally brings all of *Midnight's Children* together one more time. Throughout the novel, Rushdie has not only criticized specific instances of actions by East and West, embraced and rejected different forms of literature, interrogated concepts of gender and identity, and investigated the Indian nation, but he has also exposed the difficulty of even using any of these categories to comprehend the world. At the end of the novel, he adds one more category to this fundamental subversion: history. History is generally conceived as the exact representation of facts that happen in the real world, whereas literature is considered as stories made up of invented events. Rushdie shows, however, that there is not so much difference between the two—in Grass' native language German, for instance, *Geschichte* can mean both story and history. According to Rushdie, traditional history is written only by the dominant parts of culture and excludes groups that do not fit into the main thrust. To be more specific, for instance, the sterilization program during the Emergency is portrayed as a positive event in Indian history, whereas those who disagree with it are silenced not just themselves, but—because they can no longer reproduce—for all posterity.

Against this silence, Rushdie and Saleem write their tales. In these stories, which are also histories, factual correctness is not so important: Saleem accepts, for example, that "[t]he assassination of Mahatma Gandhi occurs, in these pages, on the wrong date" (12/189f.), and Rushdie has written an entire essay—"'Errata': or, Unreliable Narration in *Midnight's Children*," in *Imaginary Homelands*—on the topic. Instead, gossip is an acceptable form of communication, and the interpretation of a particular event is more important. When Saleem continues the preceding passage to say that, "in my India, Gandhi will continue to die at the wrong time" (12/190), Rushdie is suggesting that Gandhi's absence in India after Independence, and the subsequent loss of his ideals of secularism and tolerance, is more significant than is the exact day he passed away. In other words, it is not so much important what *happens* in history, even though that is what Padma mostly wants, but what the events *mean*. For that reason, it makes perfect sense that Saleem wants to "end up meaning—yes, meaning—something" (1/4). This interpretation, as Lipscomb argues, also explains why Rushdie on the one hand borrows information from Wolpert's standard history of India, but on the other skews or misrepresents it.

In *Midnight's Children*, meaning—which is also history—is constructed in the interaction between writer and reader with the help of facts, but also memory. As Saleem explains, he is "the apex of an isosceles triangle, supported by twin deities, the wild god of memory and the lotus-goddess of the present" (11/170). Padma is of course the lotus-goddess, and she tries to keep Saleem's story moving forward, questions him, makes interjections, and functions as the main audience. The god of memory, on the other hand, is wild because memory is unreliable. When Padma doubts Saleem's description of the Midnight Children's Conference, he answers that he has been truthful in a specific way:

I told you the truth. . . . Memory's truth, because memory has its own special kind. It selects, eliminates, alters, exaggerates, minimizes, glorifies and vilifies also; but in the end it creates its own reality, its heterogeneous but usually coherent version of events; and no sane human being ever trusts someone else's version more than his own (15/242).

In the end, this passage sums up the powerful message of *Midnight's Children*. History, or memory, is not perfect in recounting events. It can be used for good and bad ends, for constructing such categories as East and West, nation or identity, that are used to suppress peoples, people or aspects of people's personalities. At the same time, memory can be an instrument used to celebrate parts of history or individuals. There is no correct version of truth or history, but it is mostly coherent—just like Rushdie's novel is—as long as it does not digress too much or fall into one of the narrative's unfinished stories. Anyone can, and everyone has to, choose their own version of history, and should not trust others. By this Rushdie does not mean, however, that people should never trust each other; rather, it means only that they should be critical of the way a story is represented: Indira Gandhi's version of Indian history is not particularly truthful, but neither is Saleem's. In *Imaginary Homelands*, Rushdie puts it even more bluntly: "[L]iterature can, and perhaps must, give the lie to official facts" (14). Instead of allegedly historic facts, people should trust their instincts and senses, which form another leitmotif in the novel. Like Padma in *Midnight's Children*, the individual has to question whatever version of history he or she is presented with and construct their own. If everyone in India, or in the entire world, can do that, Rushdie believes, the promise of the Midnight's Children might be fulfilled after all.

3

The Novel's Reception

Publication

According to different sources, Rushdie began work on *Midnight's Children* between 1975 and 1977. The first sentence of the original manuscript was, "Most of what matters in your life takes place in your absence," and the first draft was told in the third rather than the first person. As Rushdie's agent, Liz Calder, had moved from publisher Gollancz to Jonathan Cape (a house known for its emphasis on "high" literature) since the publication of his first novel *Grimus*, Rushdie followed. He finished his manuscript in June 1979 and submitted it to Calder, who in turn gave it to several readers. One report strongly condemned the book, calling it "this fat ramble around Indian Rushdie's mind," but Cape's chairman Tom Maschler disagreed—he found it "a work of genius"—and finally decided to go ahead with publication. Because of a strike of dock-workers in the United Kingdom, the book first appeared at the beginning of March 1981 in the United States with Knopf (with a copyright date of 1980) and only on April 23, 1981, in Great Britain.

There are no significant differences between the British and U.S. versions of *Midnight's Children*. Spelling has been adjusted to reflect the national conventions (behaviour/behavior, theatre/theater, etc.); punctuation is changed slightly (the British prefer Mr and Mrs, for instance, whereas in the United States Mr. and Mrs. are more common); and some lines spacing the text have been added for the U.S. edition. One tiny change was made after 1984 in all editions of the novel, however, after Indira Gandhi won a lawsuit against Rushdie in the London High Court (which of course neither of the two attended). In the first version of the brief biographical description of Gandhi (28/484), there was one sentence that upset the then-prime minister of India, which concerns her husband Feroze Gandhi's death and her son Sanjay Gandhi's reaction: "It has often been said that Mrs. Gandhi's younger son Sanjay accused his mother of being responsible, through her neglect, for his father's death; and that this gave him an unbreakable hold over her, so that she became incapable of denying him anything." This sentence was removed in all later editions.

Even before its first publication, *Midnight's Children* received advance notice by the publication of an excerpt in the prestigious British magazine of new fiction, *Granta*. *Granta* titled its third issue, "The End of the English Novel," and in the introduction editor Bill Buford argued that English fiction—meaning, specifically, the middle-class novel—had arrived at a dead end. He also claimed that fiction was suffering from the fact that the publishing industry was no longer taking literature seriously, but marketing it like any other form of entertainment. Buford hoped that the novel would be "rescued" by writers from the margins, either from other parts of Great Britain or from other English-speaking countries. Buford wrote:

Current fiction is remarkable for its detachment, its refusal to be affiliated, its suspicion of the old hierarchies and authorities. . . . it is characterized by . . . experimentation in the real sense, exploiting traditions and not being wasted by them. The writer today is managing to reassert the act of narration—the telling not simply of fictions but stories—not in deference to the referential workings of bourgeois realism, but as an instance of the human imagination. In the work of many writers, and, here, particularly in that of Hoban and Tennant and especially Salman Rushdie, we are moving closer to the fiction of Gabriel Marquez or Italo Calvino, a magic realism, rising out of an age of technical exhaustion, where telling is at the centre of our consciousness.

The English novel has been characterized by the self-depictions of its maker's dominance: the novel of sense and sensibility is informed by the authority of belonging. Today, however, the imagination resides along the peripheries; it is spoken through a minority discourse, with the dominant tongue re-appropriated, re-commanded, and importantly re-invigorated. It is, at last, the end of the English novel and the beginning of the British one.

A section from *Midnight's Children* led the literary selection of the issue, which also included writing by Angela Carter, Desmond Hogan, Alan Sillitoe, Emma Tenant, and Russell Hoban. The passage from Rushdie's novel was the first chapter starting from Aadam Aziz's story and all of Chapter Two (1–2/4–35).

Reviews

Critic Aleid Fokkema argues that there are three aspects to the reception of Rushdie's work. His novels, she claims, are mostly either located in the Western postmodern literary tradition, or reviewers notice exotic Indian details in what theorist Edward Said has characterized as "orientalism." According to Said, Western culture has established itself as hegemonic over all other cultures—either since the eighteenth century, or always—and has not perceived the cultures of the rest of the world on their own terms. Instead, the West predetermines criteria and categories in which other, inferior cultures can portray themselves, and denies any other representations. In the process, the literature of these cultures becomes peripheral and derivative of Western—or in the case of India, English—literature. Fokkema complains, however, that even though most critics see postmodernism or exoticism, few recognize the third, political dimension of Rushdie's work.

In the actual reviews of *Midnight's Children*, however, only parts of Fokkema's theory are borne out. The most striking aspect of the reviews was certainly their general enthusiasm. In early, prepublication reviews, *Kirkus* called the novel "dizzying with talent," *Publishers Weekly* decreed the author "a writing talent to be reckoned with," and *Library Journal* found the book "one of the most intriguing narratives of recent fiction." In a review on the first page of the *New York Times Book Review*, Clark Blaise coined the phrase that was subsequently most frequently used to promote the novel: "'Midnight's Children' sounds like a continent finding its voice." On the book review page of the daily *New York Times*, John Leonard chimed in with his praise, "This novel—exuberant, excessive, despairing—is special."

On the other side of the Atlantic, critics were equally effusive. The earliest British reviews in the *Guardian* (Hilary Bailey) and the *Times* (Elaine Feinstein), respectively, found Rushdie's novel "full of life, colour, and poetry and the love, and dread, of country" (presumably India) and gushed that "I haven't been so continuously surprised by a novel since I first read *One Hundred Years of Solitude*," setting the tone for comparisons with South American magic realism. The *Financial Times* (Martin Seymour-Smith) called *Midnight's Children* "a huge and resourceful book," the *Sunday Times* (Victoria Glendinning) "a long, prolix, eccentric, brilliant piece of writing," and the *Observer* (Hermione Lee), "a magnificent book, and Salman Rushdie . . . a major novelist."

Written by another novelist of Indian origin living in the West, Anita Desai's lengthy review in the *Washington Post Book World* was the first and perhaps most insightful of all reviews in the United

States. Like many critics after her, Desai emphasizes that Rushdie was writing "a full portrait" of India, adding that he means the Subcontinent rather than just the country. Desai also picks up on one of the major tensions in the novel in that she "hesitates to call the novel 'historical' for Rushdie believes . . . that while individual history does not make sense unless seen against its national background, neither does national history make sense unless seen in the form of individual lives and histories." Although Desai worries that some readers might be put off by Rushdie's harsh satire, she argues that it is tempered by "the gift of love" for his characters and material. She points out that even though there is an element of national allegory in *Midnight's Children*, it is just as universal as the work of Cervantes, Swift, or Grass. In conclusion, Desai writes that the book "will surely be recognized as a great tour de force, a dazzling exhibition of the gifts of a new writer of courage, impressive strength, the power of both imagination and control and sheer stylistic brilliance." In other words, in terms of Fokkema's categories, Desai recognizes both Indian detail and postmodern tradition, but also insists on political resonances. Desai's opinion was also disseminated in India when her comments were republished, in slightly modified form, in the New Delhi *Book Review*.

Toward the end of her review, Desai worried about the reception of Rushdie's novel in India, writing that "it is tragic to think how unlikely that [*Midnight's Children*] will be published, distributed, or read in a land that prefers to avert its eyes from the intolerable reality." Desai was correct about an Indian *publication* of the book, but fortunately wrong about the general reception. Although slightly later in their responses—since the book had to be imported—most Indian newspapers agreed with Western assessments. In May 1981 the weekly *India Today* (Sunil Sethi) praised the expansiveness of *Midnight's Children* as "both speedy and slow, a laugh and a litany, obscure yet obvious, weird but wonderful." This review, the first in an Indian periodical and the first published interview with Rushdie anywhere, already pointed out that "foreign reviewers are so hot" on *Midnight's Children*. The New Delhi *Sunday Standard* described the novel as "an extraordinary saga of epic dimensions and resonances," and the *Patriot* (Purabi Banerjee) appreciated its "many sidedness" and called it "delectable." In October, the *Indian Express* devoted the entire first page of its magazine section to an extended excerpt titled "Love in Bombay," which was introduced with the quote from the *New York Times* mentioned above and another one from Anita Desai. In December, the *India Magazine* (Raj Thapar) offered another enthusiastic review: "While Salman Rushdie rubs out the tenuous line between fantasy and reality which is disconcerting to begin with, through the apparent jumble appears a statement which moves one both with its profundity and its compassion." The same month, the *Times of India* (N.J. Nanporia) concluded, "the dexterity of this performance, leading from one improbability to another is impressive."

Still, Desai and other reviewers found small problems with *Midnight's Children*. For Desai, the novel was "sprawling and untidy" and "the last third of the book reveals a slight dwindling of the creative spring," but these critiques were immediately contextualized as hardly noticeable in the work as a whole. The scope of *Midnight's Children* certainly seemed to pose the greatest problem for critics: One review found it "convoluted," another "overwritten." Like Desai, the *New York Times* notes a purported flaw—"Of course there are a few false notes. There is a shorter, purer novel licked inside this shaggy monster. A different author might have teased it out, a different editor might have insisted upon it"—only to add, "I'm glad they didn't." Robert Taubman in the *London Review of Books* claimed that "there are no rounded, complete characters in this novel, and Saleem's ambiguities are an aspect of the uncertainty of identity common to everyone." Even though some other critics

echoed the first complaint, the second allowed for conflicting inter-
pretations: Some believed that Saleem's commonality actually made
him universal, and therefore heightened the appeal of the novel. In
the Indian reviews, the *Times of India* found the novel "exasperat-
ing" and complained, "It screams significance but its surrealistic ex-
tensions of meaning are not convincing though offered as
significant." The *Sunday Standard* was disappointed that "one looks
[in vain] for the values that motivate Saleem's quest," and Supriya
Chaudhuri in the *Statesman* found the "insistent historical links, the
symbolic reverberations [between Saleem and India are] more irritating than not." Like Desai, Chaudhuri believed that the last third
of the novel was "much less convincing."

Nevertheless, there are no clear distinctions between reviews
from the United States, Great Britain, and India. (If anything, it is
notable that the notices in the United Kingdom were mostly in
multibook reviews, whereas those in the United States were devoted
exclusively to Rushdie's book; however, that was much more a function of newspaper practices than of assessments of the novel. There
is also no truth to the claim that Indian reviews were more critical
than were Western ones. Instead, on all three continents newspaper
reviews were generally very positive, whereas later commentary in
academic journals, appearing up to three years after the novel's publication, was more critical. In India, *Midnight's Children* was discussed in detail by such journals as *Aside* [S. Krishnan] and *New
Quest* [D.R. Sharma, R.B. Rao, M.L. Raina, R. Syal, Deval Dharkar]
as late as December 1982.) As the praise was pretty much unani-
mous, so was the interpretation of the novel: Almost all critics agreed
that the main subject of *Midnight's Children* was Indian history. In
the *New York Times Book Review* in the United States, the review
was titled, "A Novel of India's Coming of Age"; in Britain, the *Sunday Times* opined that Saleem's "story is the story of modern India";
on the Subcontinent, the *Patriot* called the novel "the history of the

country." Some critics were more careful in their analysis of *Midnight's Children* with regard to the specific genre: In the clearest terms, many saw the novel as an allegory; more carefully or with different emphases in their readings, others used such terms as epic, comic novel, picaresque, or opera buffa. In the British *New Statesman*, Bill Buford—who had previously featured Rushdie in his literary journal *Granta*—gave a range of options: "part comedy, romance, social history, and political polemic." The Indian *Sunday Standard* similarly offered, "a family saga, an allegory, a political satire, a fantasy, and a vastly comic expression of serious purpose."

Beyond the resonances between Indian history and Saleem's biography, which almost all reviews emphasized, some critics saw other issues at work in the novel. In one of the most perceptive early reviews, John Leonard in the *New York Times* was the first to use the term *fragmentation* to describe *Midnight's Children*, explaining the scope of his concept "from the sheet with the hole in it through which Saleem's grandfather is permitted to glimpse portions of the body of the woman he will marry, all the way to a dismembering of history." Leonard was also the first to recognize the metafictional nature of Rushdie's book, calling it "an exercise in criticism." Valentine Cunningham, in the *Times Literary Supplement*, saw something similar in the novel, pointing out that part of its agenda was "the business of being a novel at all." This, the review goes on to explain, is not so much an Indian disease as "a novelist's disease, but one to be opened up for inspection, foregrounded as they say."

On all three continents, critics picked up on the formal novelty of *Midnight's Children* by comparing Rushdie with South American magic realism, particularly that of Gabriel García Márquez—as Buford had already done in his introduction to *Granta*. The most frequent other literary comparison was to Günter Grass and his *Tin Drum*—so Rushdie was indeed placed in a postmodern and mostly Western (if that applies to South America) tradition, as Fokkema claims. He was, however, also likened to other Indian writers (Desai herself, Ved Mehta, and V. S. Naipaul) and to the carnivalesque traditions of Cervantes and Rabelais. Still other commentators found resemblances to such Eastern literature as Scheherazade and the *Arabian Nights*, whereas others were reminded of such Western colonial authors as Forster and Kipling. Finally, some reviewers picked up on resonances from eighteenth-century British literature and the works of Sterne, Swift, Fielding, and Pope—significant because of the origin of orientalism in the eighteenth century, according to one reading of Said's work.

The reviews of *Midnight's Children* do show some instances of the orientalism Fokkema sees in the reception of Rushdie's work. To these critics—Fokkema gives Maria Cuoto's review in the British magazine *Encounter* as a paradigmatic example—India is a unified realm that is remarkable for its exotic and mysterious nature. Its inhabitants are filthy and passive, and the country is timeless. Authors from the Indian subcontinent are supposed to represent their country in this particular way, and they are supposed to situate their writing in relation to the superior literature from the British home country. On the other hand, they expect particular insight into India from the books under consideration, which leads them to such claims as the *Sunday Times'* idea that *Midnight's Children* is "in all senses a fantastic book" as well as "an important one for Europeans to read."

Two reviews particularly guilty of an orientalist perception, although not necessarily unable to comprehend Rushdie's novel, appeared in the United States' *Newsweek* and Britain's *London Review of Books*. For *Newsweek's* critic Charles Michener, *Midnight's Children* was an unmitigated success: He called the novel "marvelous" and "extraordinary." In the process, however, he made some striking generalizations about India. First of all, he asserted that it was "the most complicated place on earth," which supposedly was reflected in the novel. Furthermore, he argued that the book "enacts . . . the tragicomedy of what it means to be Indian," apparently assuming that there was one specific way to be Indian, and that that was tragicomic. Finally, Michener probably meant his final assessment that *Midnight's Children* was "as rich as India herself" as a compliment, but essentialized the country as some kind of variegated multitude in a way that, say, the United States is not. In the *London Review of Books*, Taubman summarizes the double-edged sword of orientalism by saying that on the one hand, "Western readers were dazzled by the book's sheer foreignness" whereas, on the other, "they were astonished that material so alien could be delivered with such Westernized panache."

Another striking aspect of the first reviews of *Midnight's Children*—which might be explained by orientalism—is the astounding number of factual errors in them, both in terms of the text and in terms of history. In the *New York Times Book Review*, one of Rushdie's most perceptive and knowledgeable reviewers, Anita Desai, inexplicably claims that Saleem "is born, along with 580 babies, on the stroke of midnight on August 15, 1947." For one thing, she gets the origin of the Midnight's Children wrong: They are actually born in the first *hour* after midnight, and only Saleem and Shiva on the stroke. For another, Desai misrepresents the children in that actually 1,001 are *born* and 581 *survive*—an error that Bill Buford makes in the *New Statesman* as well. Other mistakes include *Publishers Weekly*'s statement that *Midnight's Children* is Rushdie's "brilliant debut" as well as creative misspellings of characters names, such as "Padman" (*Observer*) and "Patma" (*New York Times*) for Saleem's muse and wife. Worst of all, in the *Guardian* Bailey wrote that Saleem is born, and India becomes independent, in 1946. None of the reviewers attempt to appeal to Rushdie's apparent disregard of "truth" as excuses for imprecision, so they are certainly subject to criticism in this respect. There is of course no way to know whether these mistakes are the author's or the copy editor's fault, but perhaps they indicate a lack of knowledge particularly about matters relating to India—there is no reason to get the date of Independence wrong, and Padma is hardly an unusual name in an Indian context.

Even Indian reviews are prone to some of the generalizations about India that Said and Fokkema would characterize as orientalism. The *Sunday Standard*, for instance, even while criticizing Rushdie for not capturing it, affirms the existence of "the essential content of the reality of India," and concludes the review by conceding that "Rushdie's form and language give shape to the vastness and variety of India." As India is often associated with food in the West, the *Statesman* points out that "Rushdie has a nose for the smell of domesticity." Although it might be argued that these Indian critics have merely succumbed to the orientalism of the West, it is probably equally valid to say that it is simply impossible to write book reviews without some generalization about the work under consideration and the subject matter at hand. Whereas orientalism was certainly prevalent through most of nineteenth- and twentieth-century European writing about the East, it is difficult to convict critics of it on the strength of a short book review. Furthermore, it is difficult even to figure out whom to indict as the *Indian Express* quotes the *New York Times* and the *Washington Post* and the *Times of India* quotes almost an entire interview from (and uses the same picture of Rushdie as) the London *Sunday Times*, whereas the reviewers in the *Washington Post*, *World Literature Written in English*, *World Literature Today*, and the *Wilson Quarterly*, respectively, are the eminent Indian novelist Desai, the Ugandan writer Peter Nazareth, the Indian critic K. B. Rao, and the Indian novelist Nayantara Sahgal. Thus, in terms of Fokkema's second category, the exociting of India may be present, but it is too simple to reduce it to Western orientalism.

Reading the reviews of *Midnight's Children*, one wonders how Fokkema comes to her third claim, that Western audiences do not take sufficient notice of Rushdie's political agenda. Indian newspapers certainly did notice this dimension. *India Today*, for instance, called the book "one of the most ferocious indictments of India's evolution since Independence," and the *Sunday Standard* quoted Rushdie saying, "I wanted to get away from the family saga aspect and Book III is a deliberate change of tone; it's a much darker kind of writing and more directly political." On the other hand, another Indian newspaper, the *Patriot*, did not want to understand the *Midnight's Children* as mostly political, offering that "Rushdie is careful not to let the political angle tile the artistic side of the novel." Nanporia in the *Times of India* similarly found that "Saleem–Rushdie's political observations [are not] very profound or original. In fact they are naïve which does not matter because *Midnight's Children* is not a political tract."

At the same time, plenty of Western critics emphatically addressed the political dimension of *Midnight's Children*. There were certainly reviews such as that in the *Saturday Review* (Phyllis Birnbaum) that primarily saw the book as "a tale of family, superstition, love, belief cherished and last," then added as an afterthought, "It is also about the Indian subcontinent," and never mentioned politics—but these were unusual. It was more typical, Valentine Cunningham wrote in the *Times Literary Supplement*, for example, that the novel was characterized by "fierce political despairs and indignation" and went on to particularize them as "corruption, despotism, and carnage." Politics therefore was not only mentioned, but the reviewer interpreted these politics to be critical and pessimistic. Bill Buford argued in the *New Statesman* that Rushdie "writes a new kind of fiction of the highest order: magical, artistic, urgently political." In other words, he noticed a political perspective, and made that a prerequisite for calling the novel one of highest quality. It is hardly correct, therefore, to say like Fokkema that, "In the critical reception of *Midnight's Children* . . . political and satirical aspects have been largely overlooked in favor of the comic fantasy full of literary games and the specific 'Indianness' critics sought and found in the texts."

Beyond his definition of literary criteria, Buford also offered what he considered the political message of *Midnight's Children*: "You cannot separate the individual from the environment." Even though there can hardly be any argument over the presence of that message in Rushdie's book, it is debatable whether it really constitutes politics, and that is perhaps the root of Fokkema's problem: She seems to understand politics in the sense of party politics or specific issues and agendas, whereas *Midnight's Children* engages with politics on a more philosophical level. There is, of course, one very specific point that Rushdie drives home with great force, and which many critics noticed—his criticism of Indira Gandhi and her politics. In addition, Rushdie definitely has a bone to pick with colonialism. As a matter of fact, these are the first two points that John Leonard mentions in the *New York Times* review with sufficient humility in his introductory clause: "If I understand Rushdie, he is equally outraged by (1) the English imposition on India; (2) Indira Gandhi's 'Emergency,' which did away with liberal democracy in India." The main political thrust of *Midnight's Children*, however, is not a critique of a particular program or an endorsement of a specific candidate, but the promotion of a democratic, humanist liberalism against totalitarian ideologies, whether they be Eastern or Western, Indian or British, Gandhi or Thatcher. Because Fokkema can only recognize politics in its more programmatic incarnations, she cannot see the political commentary that Western as well as Eastern critics include in their reviews of Rushdie's novels.

In other words, Fokkema's categories of style, content, and message are certainly helpful in understanding the periodical reviews of

Midnight's Children, but her assessment of those categories goes astray. Most critics emphasize that Rushdie is writing in a formal tradition that owes much to Western literature, and they highlight the similarity of his novel to the South American genre of magic realism. Furthermore, they recognize the close proximity of the novel's "autobiographical" narrative and Indian history, often reading *Midnight's Children* as an allegory. In the process, Western critics occasionally fall prey to orientalist stereotypes, but so do Eastern reviewers of the novel. In any case, the categories of "Western" and "Eastern" are highly problematic in the context of contemporary newspaper writing and the contemporary academic scene with its migrants in positions all over the world. Finally, in contrast to what Fokkema argues, it appears that reviewers from all three countries under consideration here (i.e., the United States, Great Britain, and India) recognize the political dimension of Rushdie's novel; however, the novel is not so much interested in specific political programs, which means that to say, "*Midnight's Children* has a political message," is not to endorse a particular idea or individual.

Booker Prize

Despite the critical praise given out by the British and U.S. press—"more accolades within a month of its publication than most novels are credited with in a lifetime," as *India Today* put it as early as May 16—*Midnight's Children* had little immediate commercial success. Only 650 copies of the first print run of 2,500 books were ordered in advance, and only about 2,200 had been sold by September. Sales were even slower in the United States.

The fortunes of the book changed—at least in Great Britain—when the shortlist for the Booker McConnell Prize, Great Britain's most prestigious literary award, was announced on September 11 and included *Midnight's Children*. By October 16, Rushdie's book had sold 3,446 copies—about one thousand in one month. The other novels on the short list were Molly Keane, *Good Behaviour*; Doris Lessing, *The Sirian Experience*; Ian McEwan, *The Comfort of Strangers*; Ann Schlee, *Rhine Journey*; Muriel Spark, *Loitering with Intent*; and D. M. Thomas, *The White Hotel*. In the weeks after the announcement, commentators assumed the choice would be either Rushdie's or Thomas's book, and Rushdie's publisher Cape accordingly ordered a second printing. The London *Times* called Rushdie the "favourite" and asserted, "He has everything to gain by winning and the prize would certainly change his life." In the same article, Rushdie himself is quoted at length:

My first reaction [on hearing about *Midnight's Children* being on the shortlist] was one of relief. I would have been disappointed if it hadn't got on the short list. Before the book was published I would never have thought of such a thing. . . . I half expected it would be slammed, but the reviews were so gratifying and so many people told me it had a chance to the Booker shortlist, that I had allowed myself to think yes, it *might* be possible. I suppose it will make the public take me fractionally more serious, but it won't change the way I write.

On October 20, Rushdie indeed received the Booker Prize for 1981, which came with £10,000 of prize money. (The novel also received the venerable James Tait Black Memorial Prize and the prestigious English-Speaking Union Literary Award that year.) According to Malcolm Bradbury, the chairman of the judges for the Booker Prize, *Midnight's Children* was "a brilliant experimental novel, but also a very funny book." Furthermore, Bradbury added, it was "an extraordinary political novel." The award was noted not just in Britain, but in India as well, where both the Delhi *Times of India* and the Calcutta *Amrita Bazar Patrika*, which had not previously reviewed the novel, ran items on November 1. In addition to the critical acclaim and prize money, however, the Booker Prize from the early 1980s onward also meant a significant increase in book sales, partly because the competition between the likes of Thomas and Rushdie added to its allure. In the four weeks after receiving the prize, about eight thousand copies of *Midnight's Children* were sold, and in the weeks leading up to Christmas, another two thousand every week. At that time, the book was appearing on most British newspapers' lists of books of the year.

Rushdie hit the headlines again in December 1981 when he received a grant of £7,500 from the British Council "to assist writers of outstanding talent to work on a specific project for a concentrated period of time." Although Rushdie offered not to accept the award, the Arts Council insisted the money was for future writing, whereas they considered the Booker Prize an award for past work. In any case, by January 22, 1982, more than twenty thousand copies of *Midnight's Children* had been sold. Shortly thereafter, the print run for the paperback edition was set at forty-five thousand. Still, at the same time only seven thousand copies had been sold in the United States, perhaps a testament to Great Britain's closer connection to former colony India. Readers there had to make due with a pirated version or had to import *Midnight's Children* from abroad.

4

The Novel's Performance

Critical Commentary

For the years following its publication in 1981, *Midnight's Children* continued to experience good sales, and more than 100,000 copies had been sold in hardcover by 1990. Even more copies were sold in paperback, and of course the sales of Rushdie's books rose dramatically after the affair over *The Satanic Verses* had started. Despite *The Satanic Verses*, however, *Midnight's Children* has had the greatest literary and popular impact of all of Rushdie's novels. The novel completely changed the British perception of the Booker Prize, and of the Empire. On the one hand, with the competition between Rushdie's and Thomas's books, the prize contributed more significantly to the novel's notoriety and success than any other Booker Prize before. As a result, the press and British culture at large began paying more attention to the competition, and the prize ceremony is now even televised.

On the other hand, even though Paul Scott had won the prize in 1977 with his nostalgic book on India *Staying On*, after Rushdie's book it was clear that the view of the former colonized subjects was more important than the opinions of the colonizers. Thus, Rushdie gave a voice to writers from the Indian subcontinent, whether they were writing back home or in the British, United States, or Canadian diaspora. As a matter of fact, Indian literature since 1980 is now occasionally divided into two major categories, the more experimental followers of Rushdie and the more realistic writers, such as Vikram Seth. For that reason, a younger generation including such Anglo-Indian writers as Vikram Chandra, Shashi Tharoor, and even Rohinton Mistry is sometimes called "Rushdie's children."

Not all critics see Rushdie's influence on Anglo-Indian literature as positive. For example, Pankaj Mishra—editor at Penguin India and an author himself—has complained that Rushdie's prominence was obscuring the excellent output of Indian writers in such native languages as Hindi, Marathi, Bengali, and Malayam. Furthermore, Mishra is unhappy about the "set of defective clones" imitating Rushdie. Nevertheless, even he calls the newest generation of writers in English from the Subcontinent (i.e., Amitav Ghosh, Mukul Kesavan, Arundhati Roy, Amit Chaudhuri, Raj Khamal Jha, Kiran Desai) "Midnight's grandchildren."

The excellence of *Midnight's Children* was confirmed critically once more in 1993 when the Booker Prize committee decided to celebrate its twenty-fifth anniversary by choosing the best of the past twenty-five winners—and selected Rushdie's book. Although there may have been a political dimension to the decision—the author was still in hiding, and the campaign to support him was in full swing—the three judges praised the book mainly in literary terms. Malcolm Bradbury, once again chair of the panel of judges, called *Midnight's Children* "the richest expression of the variety and depth of the contemporary fictional imagination, a flamboyant, experimental celebration of the power and potential of human narrative." David Holloway wrote that the novel was "a breaker of new ground, not only in the way that it presents the India of the immediate postwar period but in its method of narration, the mixing in of a certain magical element echoing the work of South American novelists."

Finally, W. L. Webb added that Rushdie's book was "a work which extended yet again the sense of the novel's possibilities, and changed the way we understand a violently changing world."

There has similarly been no limit to accolades for *Midnight's Children* within academic scholarship. First, and perhaps most obviously, Rushdie's novel is credited with a re-invigoration of the English novel in India. Viney Kirpal, for instance, distinguishes three phases in the Indian novel between 1930 and 1980 (i.e., historical, sociopolitical, and psychological) with *Midnight's Children* inaugurating a fourth phase: "With the publication of *Midnight's Children* in 1980, the Indian English Novel changed course . . . [it] had entered the phase of the postmodern novel." In addition, the book for the first time presented a specifically Indian form of the English language in writing, allowing authors to capture a new kind of voice. Like Kirpal, many subcontinental critics believe that Rushdie inspired an entire new generation of authors to write in English. *Midnight's Children* has influence beyond just India, however, infusing much literature from the former colonies with South American ideas. The *Oxford Companion to Twentieth-Century Literature in English*, for instance, claims, "This highly innovative novel was the forerunner of a new genre of writing from India, other Asian countries, and Africa, combining the magic realism of Latin American novels with political comment, satire, and dissertations on contemporary history in the context of decolonization."

In more general terms—and relocated geographically—Randall Stevenson calls *Midnight's Children* "one of the most impressive and significant novels of the eighties" in his *Reader's Guide to the Twentieth-Century Novel in Britain* (136). Most strongly, Michael Wood gives Rushdie's book credit for changing the course of literature in Great Britain altogether in his essay, "The Contemporary Novel," in the authoritative *Columbia History of the British Novel*. According to Wood, "[t]he 1980s witness an astonishing rebirth of storytelling in British fiction," and the writer most responsible for this change was Rushdie, "whose *Midnight's Children* . . . effected a massive, garrulous liberation in British fiction."

Nevertheless, there is at least one ongoing critical controversy over Salman Rushdie and his *Midnight's Children*, that of the question of the novel's politics. To some querulous writers, the success of the book is based less on its literary quality, and more on the fact that it offers exotic landscapes to Western readers and assuages the colonial guilt of Western liberal critics by pretending to be Indian. According to this model, Rushdie is complicit with the exploitation of such subaltern cultures and economies as India by global capitalism, and his novels are no more than interesting escapist fantasies; however, there is a significant problem with this attack: It seems to be based entirely on the critics' political agendas rather than on Rushdie's text. On the one hand, these critics can claim that *Midnight's Children* draws on an Eastern tradition, which it merely exoticizes for Western audiences; on the other, they can locate the book in Western traditions of magic realism or Menippean satire, in which case Rushdie is a sell-out. At the same time, however, those very same traditions can be interpreted quite differently—as an embrace of Eastern literary forms as a challenge to the West, or an undermining of Western traditions to subvert capitalist hegemony— and few critics bother enough with the actual words on the page to make their case.

Movie Adaptation

Rushdie describes the process of trying to turn his most famous book into a movie in the essay, "Adapting Midnight's Children," originally published as "Midnight Cowboys" in the *Sunday Times* and later included as an introduction to the 1999 British publication of the screenplay. It was more recently republished, with a few alterations, in *Step Across This Line*. Because the attempt to turn the novel into a television event had been sabotaged by political interests in 1999, Rushdie then called the publication of the screenplay a "small gesture of defiant utterance" and wanted his work "to be on the record, publicly available to be judged, not just in the courts of political expediency, but by the public at large." By 2002, the year of the essay collection, the series had still not been produced, but Rushdie was more optimistic, as he details in an endnote.

Rushdie recounts that immediately after the publication of *Midnight's Children* in 1981, two directors approached him about a film version; however, the first project "never got off the ground," and the author rejected the second because the director wanted to cut the section dealing with the Emergency as "really unnecessary." After the novel received the Booker of Bookers in 1993, Rushdie was approached by Britain's BBC and Channel Four, and chose the former for the adaptation. Because he did not want to write the script himself, Ken Taylor was drafted for that purpose; however, when various directors, producers, and Rushdie himself subsequently kept changing the shape of the project, Taylor withdrew and the author decided to contribute the script himself after all. According to Rushdie, that finally happened in "a mad writing burst. In five weeks in November and December 1996, I finished a draft of the entire five-episode screenplay." The broadcast was supposed to last 290 minutes.

In contrast to Taylor, Rushdie writes, "I was much less respectful of the original text . . ." The author made significant changes: "Out went long sequences . . . Out went some of the novel's more fanciful notions (a politician who literally hummed with energy) and peripheral characters (the snake-poison expert who lives upstairs from the Sinai family). In came new devices, such as the idea of allowing the peep-show man, Lifafa Das, to introduce each episode as if it were a part of his peep show." For instance, the second episode begins with Das shouting, "Come see India, come see Pakistan, come see!/ Come see one child, long-while exiled,/Loss of innocence, come see!/Come see come see come see!" Furthermore, Rushdie changed story lines to fit the structure of a television miniseries. Most importantly, in the relationship between Saleem and Shiva, "on the screen . . . so large a plot motif simply insists on a climactic confrontation, and so I have provided one." In this confrontation in the fifth episode, where Shiva personally arrests Saleem and takes him to the prison in the widows' hostel, Saleem tells his captor, "You're really me. I'm really you." Shiva's reaction is expressed through facial expressions rather than words: *"On Shiva's face we see understanding beginning to dawn./Followed by an attempt to conceal the understanding./Followed by rage."* After this brief refusal and subsequent reaction, Shiva says to Saleem, "Bastard. Haramzada."—the same word in English and Hindi.

Happy with the project at this stage, Rushdie and director Tristram Powell ran into the next problem: money. Two private investors of Indian origin secured financing, however, and casting began in London and Bombay. In contrast to a generation earlier, Rushdie writes, "we were able to audition a diverse and multitalented throng" of Asian actors. Some established Indian actors were asked to choose their own roles, and others (e.g., Rahul Bose as Saleem) were "discovered." The project unfortunately finally floundered—not just once, but twice—on politics. After casting, it turned out the Indian government had refused permission for filming, perhaps fearing unrest if Rushdie returned to India. Instead, Sri Lanka initially approved the project in 1997—but then had to withdraw in November after journalists stirred up Muslim members of parliament. Rushdie compares the process to a Greek mythological figure: "Like Sisyphus, we had to watch the undoing of all of our work, as the great rock of our production ran away downhill into a Sri Lankan ditch."

Dramatic Adaptation

Nevertheless, the work for the cinematic adaptation of *Midnight's Children* was not entirely in vain. Rushdie used his script several years later as the starting point for a stage adaptation by the Royal Shakespeare Company. This dramatization premiered in London on January 29, 2003, briefly visited Michigan and New York, and then returned for a successful tour of Great Britain in the spring and summer, 2003. It has also been released as a book.

In this version, directed by Tim Supple, with dramaturge Simon Reade, with a three-and-a-half-hour running time, Saleem writes and tells his story while other members of the cast of 20 (i.e., with most playing more than one role) enact them. In the background, newsreels supply a historical context that replaces much of the detail of the novel—perhaps a relic of the film adaptation. For instance, in the opening scene, Nehru's "Tryst with Destiny" speech is playing while Saleem and Shiva are born. (The program notes include a family tree to avoid confusion in the audience.) The play also employs such other media as specially filmed scenes—some of which the real-life actors later interact with on stage—and play with shadows. At the announcement of Gandhi's death, for example, the actors in a Bollywood movie that Saleem is watching break out of their role to react to the news. In another scene, Parvati and Shiva are visible and speak on a cinema screen, but act on the stage at the same moment. The climactic confrontation between Saleem and Shiva at the prison of the widows' hostel still exists with the same words, but now the stage direction is one step shorter: Shiva is merely *"enraged as it dawns on him."*

The reception of the play was mixed. Even though critics unanimously lauded the general attempt to bring such a sprawling text to the stage, some were unsatisfied with the result. In the *Guardian*, Michael Billington wrote, "This version does manage to capture something of the novel's narrative abundance," and called the show, "an evening of memorable moments." The *Times* (Benedict Nightingale) summarized that this was "a bold, lively effort, but, more than any stage adaptation I know, it leaves you hankering for the page." The *Independent*'s Paul Taylor was most critical, describing the evening as "only a very partial success." All reviews, however, particularly praised the performance of Zubin Varla, who as Saleem presents "a slightly and rightly irritating tour de force" and "is simultaneously narrator, chameleonlike changeling, historic symbol, and ruined victim of the Indira Gandhi years [who] dominates the stage." In the United States critics were less kind toward *Midnight's Children*, the play. The *New York Times* found it "thin to the point of transparency" and "stillborn," whereas the New York *Daily News* spoke of "boredom" and argued that the production "is essentially a college show." Still, it appears that after the dramatic adaptation, discussion of a film version has once again started.

5

Further Reading and Discussion Questions

Salman Rushdie

A reader who enjoys *Midnight's Children* will probably like most of Rushdie's other novels. In the course of his writing career, the locations of the novels have migrated from science fiction through India and Pakistan to Spain and London and finally to New York.

Grimus. London: Gollancz, 1975.
Shame. London: Cape, 1981.
The Satanic Verses. London: Penguin, 1988.
The Moor's Last Sigh. London: Cape, 1995.
The Ground Beneath Her Feet. London: Cape, 1999.
Fury. London: Cape, 2001.

Rushdie has also published a collection of nine short stories, some of which were previously published in various periodicals, as well as a children's book that is hardly restricted to young children.

Haroun and the Sea of Stories. London: Penguin/Granta, 1990.
East, West. London: Cape, 1994.

In addition to two versions of *Midnight's Children*, the children's book *Haroun and the Sea of Stories* has been adapted for the stage. The three scripts have all been published.

The Screenplay of Midnight's Children. London: Vintage, 1999.
Salman Rushdie's Haroun and the Sea of Stories. Adapted by Tim Supple and David Tushingham. London: Faber and Faber, 1998.
Salman Rushdie's Midnight's Children. Adapted for the Theatre by Salman Rushdie, Simon Reade and Tim Supple. London: Vintage, 2003.

Furthermore, Rushdie regularly writes nonfiction. At the beginning of his career, this work focused more on literature and on India. In July 1986, Rushdie visited Nicaragua and reflected on his experience in a travelogue. The Rushdie Affair, of course, offered endless subject material. During his "exile," Rushdie wrote a wonderful booklet on *The Wizard of Oz*, which was reprinted later in *Step Across This Line*—but unfortunately without illustrations. By the beginning of the new century, Rushdie was in demand as a political commentator in general—his columns can still be found every few weeks in such newspapers as the *New York Times* and the British *Guardian*—along with opinions on topics from soccer to photography, and movies to pop music.

The Jaguar Smile: A Nicaraguan Journey. London: Pan Books, 1987.
Imaginary Homelands. London: Penguin/Granta, 1991.
The Wizard of Oz. London: British Film Institute Publishing, 1992.
Step Across This Line. London: Cape, 2002.

Other Fiction

Readers of *Midnight's Children* will also enjoy other novels that are set in India or that use magic realism. There is an entire generation of writers in English from India who are referred to as "Rushdie's children," but of course not all of them write as does Rushdie. Some novels are concerned with Indian history, and particularly with Partition, as much as or more than *Midnight's Children*.

Baldwin, Shauna Singh. *What the Body Remembers* (1999).
Manto, Saadat Hasan. *Mottled Dawn* (1997).
Sidhwa, Bapsi. *The Ice Candy Man* (1988).
Singh, Kushwant. *Train to Pakistan* (1956).

Other novels are of interest because they employ a style similar to Rushdie's (Roy), because they try to give Indian history a fictional shape based on mythology (Tharoor), because they present a panorama of Indian society (Seth), and because they connect the Subcontinent to the United States (Lahiri) or to Great Britain (Kureishi).

Kesavan, Mukhul. *Looking Through Glass* (1995).
Kureishi, Hanif. *The Buddha of Suburbia* (1990).
Lahiri, Jhumpa. *Interpreter of Maladies* (1999).
Mistry, Rohinton. *A Fine Balance* (1996).
Roy, Arundhati. *The God of Small Things* (1997).
Seth, Vikram. *A Suitable Boy* (1993).
Tharoor, Shashi. *The Great Indian Novel* (1989).

Other literature includes influences that Rushdie has cited himself, or that critics have recognized in his writing. Some of these authors (García Márquez, Grass) are considered part of the tradition of magic realism.

García Márquez, Gabriel. *One Hundred Years of Solitude* (1967).
Grass, Günter. *The Tin Drum* (1959).
Sterne, Laurence. *Tristram Shandy* (1759–67).

On the other hand, there is the tradition of British colonial narrative about India *against* which Rushdie is writing. Both Kaye and Scott wrote series of novels set in the subcontinent.

Forster, E.M. *Passage to India* (1924).

Kaye, Mary Margaret. *The Far Pavilions* (1978).

Scott, Paul. *The Raj Quartet: The Jewel in the Crown, The Day of the Scorpion, The Towers of Silence, A Division of the Spoils* (1966–75).

Criticism

There is certainly no shortage of criticism on Rushdie in general, and on *Midnight's Children* in particular. At least one book-length bibliography on the author has been published, although it is unfortunately out of date and rather incomplete. The one authorized biography on Rushdie ends with the Rushdie Affair. A more recent article describes his first year in New York.

Hamilton, Ian. "The First Life of Salman Rushdie." *The New Yorker* 71.42 (December 25, 1995–January 1, 1996): 90–113.

Kuortti, Joel. *The Salman Rushdie Bibliography*. Frankfurt: Peter Lang, 1997.

Rushdie has expressed many of his thoughts about the book, and about a plethora of other subjects, in interviews given over the course of his life. Many of these essays have been collected in two volumes, although both are slightly outdated and need to be supplemented.

Reder, Michael (ed.). *Conversations with Salman Rushdie*. Jackson, MS: University Press of Mississippi, 2000.

Chauhan, Pradyumna (ed.). *Salman Rushdie Interviews: A Sourcebook of His Ideas*. Westport, CT: Greenwood Press, 2001.

Max, D. T. "The Concrete Beneath His Feet." *The New York Times*, September 17, 2000: magazine 68–70.

Furthermore, Rushdie himself has expressed his opinions on *Midnight's Children*, on its cinematic adaptation, and on the state of Indian literature in a number of publications. Two of those have never been collected in his nonfictional books.

"The Indian Writer in England." *The Eye of the Beholder: Indian Writing in English*. Maggie Butcher (ed.). London: Commonwealth Institute, 1983. pp. 75–83.
"Midnight Cowboys." *The Sunday Times* 9108 (March 21, 1999): 7.
"*Midnight's Children* and *Shame*." *Kunapipi* 7.1 (1985): 1–19.

The Rushdie Affair has been the subject of many books. Here are a few titles:

Abdallah, Anour (ed.). *For Rushdie: Essays by Arab and Muslim Writers in Defense of Free Speech*. New York: Braziller, 1994.
Ahsan, M. M., and A.R. Kidwai (eds.). *Sacrilege Versus Civility: Muslim Perspectives on the Satanic Verses Affair*. Markfield, UK: Islamic Foundation, 1993.
Appignanesi, Lisa, and Sara Maitland. *The Rushdie File*. London: ICA, Fourth Estate, 1989.
MacDonogh, Steve (ed. in association with Article 19). *The Rushdie Letters: Freedom to Speak, Freedom to Write*. Lincoln: University of Nebraska Press, 1993.

A number of academic critics have published their thoughts on Rushdie's literary work in book format. Most of these books include a chapter or other extensive sections devoted to *Midnight's Children*. They can be found in good public or university libraries.

Blake, Andrew. *Salman Rushdie: A Beginner's Guide*. London: Hodder & Stoughton, 2001.

Brennan, Timothy. *Salman Rushdie and the Third World: Myths of the Nation*. New York: St. Martin's, 1989.

Clark, Roger. *Stranger Gods: Salman Rushdie's Other Worlds*. Montreal: McGill-Queen's University Press, 2001.

Cundy, Catherine. *Salman Rushdie*. Manchester: Manchester University Press, 1996.

Goonetilleke, D.C.R.A. *Salman Rushdie*. New York: St. Martin's Press, 1998.

Grant, Damian. *Salman Rushdie*. Plymouth: Northcote House, in association with the British Council, 1999.

Harrison, James. *Salman Rushdie*. New York: Twayne, 1992.

Hassumani, Sabrina. *Salman Rushdie: A Postmodern Reading of His Major Works*. Madison, NJ: Fairleigh Dickinson University Press, 2002.

Parameswaran, Uma. *The Perforated Sheet: Essays on Salman Rushdie's Art*. New Delhi: Affiliated East-West Press, 1988.

Sanga, Jaina. *Salman Rushdie's Postcolonial Metaphors: Migration, Translation, Hybridity, Blasphemy, and Globalization*. Westport, CT: Greenwood Press, 2001.

At least two books are concerned more specifically with *Midnight's Children*. While one provides a reader's guide, including specific questions for students (Reynolds/Noakes), the other excerpts and evaluates reviews and criticism (Smale). There is a large body of academic literature concerned with interpreting *Midnight's Children*, but most of it is difficult to find in scholarly journals; however, there is one volume of collected essays on Rushdie's novel (Mukherjee).

Mukherjee, Meenakshi (ed.). *Rushdie's* Midnight's Children: *A Book of Readings*. Delhi: Pencraft, 1999.

Reynolds, Margaret, and Jonathan Noakes. *Salman Rushdie: The Essential Guide*. London: Vintage, 2003.

Smale, David (ed.). *Salman Rushdie: Midnight's Children/The Satanic Verses. A Reader's Guide to Essential Criticism*. Cambridge: Icon, 2001.

A few articles were particularly insightful or important to me and are referred to specifically in the text.

Booker, M. Keith. "*Midnight's Children*, History, and Complexity: Reading Rushdie after the Cold War." *Critical Essays on Salman Rushdie.* M. Keith Booker (ed.). New York: G.K. Hall, 1999: pp. 283–313.

Brennan, Tim. "Fantasy, Individuality, and the Politics of Liberation." *Polygraph* 1.1 (1987): 89–99.

Hawes, Clement. "Leading History by the Nose: The Turn to the Eighteenth Century in *Midnight's Children*." *Modern Fiction Studies* 39.1 (Winter 1993): 147–168.

Lewis, Robin Jared. "Salman Rushdie: *Midnight's Children*." *Masterworks of Asian Literature in Comparative Perspective: A Guide for Teaching.* Barbara Stoler Miller (ed.). Armonk, NY: Sharpe, 1994: pp. 178–188.

Lipscomb, David. "Caught in a Strange Middle Ground: Contesting History in Salman Rushdie's *Midnight's Children*." *Diaspora* 1.2 (Fall 1991): 163–189.

Stephens, John. "'To tell the truth, I lied . . .': Retrospectivity and Deconstruction as (Contributing) Strategies for Reading Salman Rushdie's *Midnight's Children*." *SPAN* 21 (October 1985): 193–208.

Indian History

There are several excellent books that deal with Indian history, and the two consulted for this book (Kulke/Rothermund and Metcalf/ Metcalf) as well as the one Rushdie used (Wolput) in an earlier edition are presented here. In addition, this section lists a book on the Emergency as well as an article treating the legal interaction between Rushdie and Indira Gandhi leading to the only change in the text of *Midnight's Children*.

Dhar, P.N. *Indira Gandhi, the "Emergency," and Indian Democracy.* New Delhi: Oxford University Press, 2000.

Kulke, Hermann, and Dieter Rothermund. A *History of India*. Third ed. London and New York: Routledge, 1998.

Metcalf, Barbara, and Thomas Metcalf. A *Concise History of India*. Cambridge: Cambridge University Press, 2001.

Wolpert, Stanley. A *New History of India*. Sixth ed. New York: Oxford University Press, 2000.

Before and after the success of *Midnight's Children* with awards and within the academic realm, a number of authors reflected on the conditions leading to that success as well as the ideology behind it.

Buford, Bill. "Introduction." *Granta* 3 (1980): 7–16.

Calder, Liz. "Bandwagon Blues." *The Bookseller* 3974 (February 1982): 640–642.

Davies, Hunter. "Giving the Poor Old Novel a Bit of a Boost." *The Times* 61059 (October 19, 1981): 9.

Davies, Hunter. "Heavyweight Champions." *The Sunday Times* 8223 (February 7, 1982): 13.

Fokkema, Aleid. "English Ideas of Indianness: The Reception of Salman Rushdie." *Crisis and Creativity in the New Literatures in English*. Geoffrey Davis and Hena Maes-Jelinek (eds.). Amsterdam: Rodopi, 1990. pp. 355–368.

Frank, Katherine. "Mr. Rushdie and Mrs. Gandhi." *Biography* 19.3 (Summer 1996): 245–258.

Said, Edward. *Orientalism*. New York: Pantheon, 1978.

Todd, Richard. *Consuming Fictions: The Booker Prize and Fiction in Britain Today*. London: Bloomsbury, 1996.

Performance

In recent years, *Midnight's Children* has been commented on by British, U.S.–American, and Indian writers in a variety of contexts (e.g., concerning Rushdie's influence on Indian writing, at the time of the "Booker of Bookers," and in literary histories).

"The Booker of Bookers: 25 Years of the Booker Prize." *The Times*, September 21, 1993: supplement.

Huggan, Graham. "The Postcolonial Exotic: Salman Rushdie and the Booker of Bookers." *Transition* 64 (1994): 22–29.

Kirpal, Viney (ed.). *The Postmodern Indian English Novel*. New Delhi: Allied Publishers, 1996.

Mishra, Pankaj. "Midnight's Grandchildren." *Prospect* 17 (April 1997): 54–55.

Stringer, Jenny (ed.). *Oxford Companion to Twentieth-Century Literature in English*. Oxford: Oxford University Press, 1996.

Stevenson, Randall. *A Reader's Guide to the Twentieth-Century Novel in Britain*. New York: Harvester Wheatsheaf, 1993.

Wood, Michael. "The Contemporary Novel." *Columbia History of the British Novel*. John Richetti (ed.). New York: Columbia University Press, 1994: pp. 966–987.

Discussion Questions

The most extensive list of study questions for *Midnight's Children* is available in Reynold' and Noakes' *Salman Rushdie: The Essential Guide* listed earlier. Similar but shorter lists or analyses of the novel are (currently) available online at such sites as:

- www.shsu.edu/~eng_sdg/rushdie.html
- books.rpmdp.com/rated99/rushdie.htm
- www.eng.fju/edu/tw/Literary_Criticism/postcolonism/Mid_Children.htm
- www.subir.com/rushdie.html
- www.litencyc.com

1. Rushdie could have narrated his story in a number of different formats, but chose to present it as the "autobiography" of the main protagonist. What function does the narrator Saleem Sinai have for the meaning of *Midnight's Children*?

2. Throughout *Midnight's Children*, it is sometimes difficult to see which characters were invented by Rushdie, which ones are based on historical figures, and which ones *are* actually historical. What are examples for each category? What significance do the three categories have?

3. *Midnight's Children* begins in 1915 and ends in 1978. Why does Rushdie select this particular segment of Indian history? What does the reader learn about the origin and history of India, Pakistan, and Bangladesh? What is happening in the rest of the world during this period? How is the British presence, and later legacy, in India represented?

4. On the first page of *Midnight's Children*, Saleem states that he was "mysteriously handcuffed to history, my destinies indissolubly chained to those of my country." What does this claim mean? How does Saleem develop the connection in the course of the story, and how does the narrative itself support his claim?

5. Rushdie has said in essays, lectures, and interviews that *Midnight's Children* is held together by leitmotifs. What are some of those leitmotifs, and how do they keep the novel from falling apart? What information do they provide for the interpretation of the novel?

6. There are a large number of characters that are introduced in the course of *Midnight's Children*. Are these figures presented as characters with psychological depth, as representatives of certain groups, as stereotypes, or as some combination of the preceding?

7. At the center of *Midnight's Children*, there is the group of children with that title. What do they represent? How many are there, and what is their history? Which ones play a major part in the novel? Discuss the relationship between Saleem and Shiva!

8. List the women figures in *Midnight's Children* in general, and Saleem's "mothers" in particular! How does Rushdie portray these characters? Are there specific characteristics that he reserves for women, and others for men? What significance does Padma have for the novel as a whole?

9. *Midnight's Children* is generally recognized as a part of the literary movement known as *magic realism*. Offer a definition of that term. What aspects of magic realism are present in the novel, and which are absent? Why does Rushdie include abilities or events in his novel that are physically impossible?

10. Truth and reality are not the same thing in *Midnight's Children*. What position does Saleem take toward these concepts? How does the novel tell us to evaluate them, and how does it want us to evaluate Saleem?

11. Who is the "Widow" of *Midnight's Children*? When is she first introduced, and when does the reader learn who she really is? At what points does the text refer to her? What function does she have in Saleem's biography?

12. Look at the very last paragraph of the novel:

Yes, they will trample me underfoot, the numbers marching one two three, four hundred million five hundred six, reducing me to specks of voiceless dust, just as, in all good time, they will trample my son who is not my son, and his son who will not be his, and his who will not be his, until the thousand and first generation, until a thousand and one midnights have bestowed terrible gifts and a thousand and one children have died, because it is the privilege and the curse of midnight's children to be both masters and victims of their times, to forsake privacy and be sucked into the annihilating whirlpool of the multitudes, and to be unable to live or die in peace.

Explain the situation Saleem is describing. Why is the number he gives six hundred million? Why does he fear being turned into "voiceless dust"? Why is his son not his son, and why will that pattern repeat itself in the future? Is there a reason Rushdie repeats the number 1,001 several times? In what sense do the midnight's children have a privilege and a curse? How are they "both masters and victims of their times"? Why are they "unable to live and die in peace"?

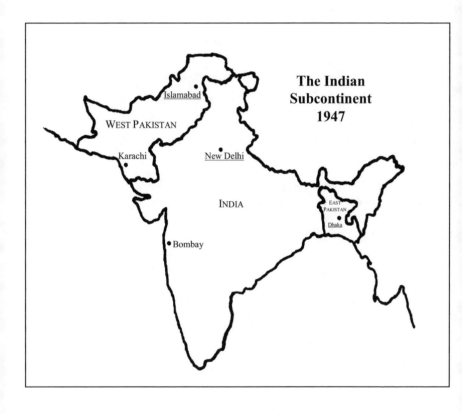

The Indian
Subcontinent
1947

WEST PAKISTAN

Islamabad

Karachi

New Delhi

INDIA

EAST
PAKISTAN

Dhaka

Bombay

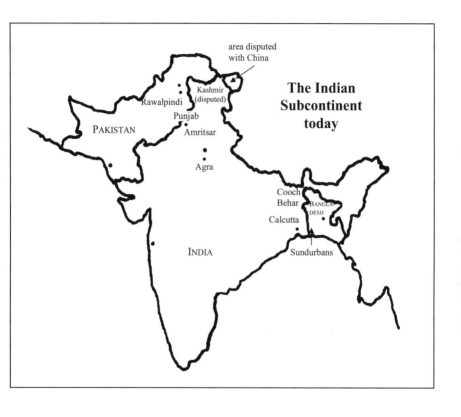

area disputed
with China

The Indian
Subcontinent
today

Kashmir
(disputed)

Rawalpindi

Punjab

PAKISTAN

Amritsar

Agra

Cooch
Behar

BANGLA-
DESH

Calcutta

INDIA

Sundurbans